T0220308

The Digital Healthcare Revolution

Martina Toni • Giovanni Mattia

The Digital Healthcare Revolution

Towards Patient Centricity with Digitization,
Service Innovation and Value Co-creation

Martina Toni
Roma Tre University
Rome, Italy

Giovanni Mattia
Roma Tre University
Rome, Italy

ISBN 978-3-031-16342-5   ISBN 978-3-031-16340-1   (eBook)
https://doi.org/10.1007/978-3-031-16340-1

This Palgrave Macmillan imprint is published by the registered company Springer Nature
Switzerland AG.
The registered company address is: Gewerbestrasse 11, 6330 Cham, Switzerland

CONTENTS

Contents

LIST OF FIGURES

LIST OF TABLES

CHAPTER 1

Introduction

Abstract This chapter provides an overview of the book's contents and the related chapters. The aim is to offer an overall framework in which the link among all the topics is highlighted. Indeed, each chapter represents a knowledge input for the subsequent ones and for building the theoretical framework.

Keywords Digitization • Service innovation • Value co-creation • Patient centricity

Service innovation affects every sector and further impacts could be expected from Industry 4.0 implementation. The healthcare sector is one of the most relevant for society, and technological application is acquiring increasing attention due to the necessity of facing growing challenges in balancing health demand and limited resources. This book deals with the potentially revolutionary effect that healthcare can benefit from technological advances. These benefits are clear from the individual (patients and healthcare professionals) to the system perspective (healthcare organizations and policymakers).

From the system perspective, healthcare organizations require to manage the growing flow of patients, provide the best care service, and avoid duplication of costs. Individuals ask for continuity of care with a customized service that is considered efficient from resources, time, and cost

M. Toni, G. Mattia, *The Digital Healthcare Revolution*,
https://doi.org/10.1007/978-3-031-16340-1_1

1

viewpoints. The starting point is enhancing information and data sharing, optimizing processes through clinicians' collaboration, patients' engagement, and remote solutions that enable seamless health services. This digital transformation implies rethinking the entire system in an open way in which the separability of the service becomes outdated and patients can easily access care services both inside hospital facilities and outside through innovative channels. Multiple aspects need to be combined together to move further to an innovative scenario: the system should be based on patient focus, value maximization, and sustainability.

This book deals with patients' experiences from a managerial perspective focusing on secondary services to the medical care of patients. However, in the future scenario, digital tools can be integrated into medical care to improve its outcomes. By following the chapters' contents, the book provides an overall framework in which the link among all the topics is highlighted. Indeed, each chapter represents a knowledge input for the subsequent ones and for building the theoretical framework. Here following, a brief description of each chapter is illustrated.

Chapter 2 focuses on digitization, which is considered a lever for a transformative process toward value co-creation and patient centricity. It represents the starting point of the book since a paradigm shift in digital technologies is occurring; indeed, Healthcare 4.0 is likely to positively impact the internal perspective (i.e., improving data flow, customizing the clinicians-patients relationship) and the patients' literacy in terms of decision-making, ability to select reliable sources of information, and interact with clinicians.

Chapter 3 illustrates the environment in which the healthcare transformation is occurring. The growing awareness on the sustainability and One Health concepts affect the healthcare sector with the aim to shed light on the relations between humans, animals, and the shared environment and its potential negative implications. Digitization supports public health by collecting a vast amount of information and tracing human and veterinary medical data in a reliable way into real-time information systems.

The necessity of integrating systems is also highlighted by the Value Agenda, which aims to move from a fragmented system to an integrated one that focuses on creating value for patients. Indeed, Chap. 4 deals with Value-Based Healthcare (VBH) and the necessity to exploit technological innovation to focus on value provided to patients consistently with their needs. Digitization can support this change by guaranteeing real-time decision-making and business continuity.

Patients should be involved in health service through a value co-creation approach (Chap. 5), allowing them to act as resource integrators and active co-creators of value in collaboration with healthcare professionals. Digitization is a lever for empowering patients by facilitating the exchange with healthcare professionals and minimizing barriers.

Chapters 6 and 7 deal with the patient focus. Chapter 6 provides a conceptual framework of patient centricity, encompassing the main definitions and steps of implementation. Patients' experience (Chap. 7) is linked to the pursuit of patient centricity and is central to redesigning the healthcare service delivery around the actual needs of patients. In order to improve the experience and focus the healthcare service on patients, the chapter examines in depth the patient journey and its touchpoints. The integration of digital health technologies into the patient journey could support healthcare systems to maintain a patient-centric view in two ways: measuring patient experience in real time and contributing to patient engagement.

Chapter 8 deals with the concept of sustainability, including patient wellbeing, Transformative Service Research (TSR), and Agenda 2030. A global strategy with successful interactions among several entities and users is crucial to realize wellbeing outcomes, decreasing disparity and enhancing health and happiness. Digitization contributes to wellbeing through continuity of care by creating more opportunities for interactions outside the physical environment; moreover, technologies can reduce the suffering of humans and society through prevention, early detection, diagnosis, remote care, telehealth, and real-time communication.

Chapter 9 proposes an overview of the entire book by building a theoretical framework on the basis of the emerged topics, highlighting the role of technology.

The healthcare revolution toward patient centricity is supported by digitization and its potential to increase the value provided to patients, the experience of care, multidirectional collaboration, and patient wellbeing. The critical turning point is a mindset shift toward the achievement of patient centricity. Digitization, service innovation, and value co-creation can contribute to this purpose as levers that change the healthcare system from reactive to proactive by monitoring patients' needs and their evolution throughout the healthcare journey. Patient centricity and patient participation in healthcare need to be the central scope of healthcare organizations since positive implications are associated in terms of medical outcomes, lower costs, more effective and efficient service delivery, increased quality and satisfaction, and personalization of healthcare.

CHAPTER 2

Healthcare in the 4.0 Era of Digitization

Abstract A paradigm shift in digital technologies is occurring in almost every sector, even though specifically in healthcare it could represent an answer to the main challenges pressing the healthcare system. The system's fragmentation due to a silos structure implies that information is not adequately integrated across facilities and territory.

Innovation through Health 4.0 is crucial to improve data flow, customize the clinicians-patients relationship through remote human touch, and focus the process on patients. From the patients' perspective, new technologies can also be used to improve the level of awareness related to health and support decision-making. Digitization is a lever to activate the transformative process aimed at overcoming the main healthcare gaps enabling value cocreation and patient centricity.

Keywords Healthcare 4.0 • Digitization • Service innovation • Innovation archetypes • Smart healthcare

The healthcare system is experiencing an unprecedented time made of challenges and opportunities that will revolutionize the sector. A paradigm shift in digital technologies is occurring, which could represent an answer to the outbreak of pandemic crisis that pressed the healthcare system, emphasizing its main criticalities.

The main criticalities of the healthcare system have been exacerbated in terms of significant fragmentation within the sector and data management, lack of interconnections and network creation, limited resources, and the need to minimize costs. The necessity to overcome these issues paves the way for opportunities to improve the system from a multidisciplinary perspective. The health system's management and monitoring need to be rethought under a novel lens to meet the growing demand due to two general trends: the extension of life expectancy and the increase in chronic diseases. Opportunities for innovative business models are emerging in order to fill the existing gaps.

The existence of different regional healthcare systems implies significant fragmentation. Thus actions are necessary to ensure uniformity of the health services and strengthen prevention and local assistance; this aim can be pursued by reinforcing integration among hospitals, local healthcare structures, and social services. The system's fragmentation implies that information is not adequately integrated across structures and territory. It has to be noted that many healthcare systems, especially in developing countries, depend mainly on paper-based processes to capture, process, and manage health data. It is increasingly becoming difficult to access, store, process, analyze, and integrate vast volumes of health data stored in paper-based health systems (Mbunge, 2020). As a consequence, actions should be undertaken to guarantee access to services and care, transparency of information, communication and integration of data with the involvement of patients and the support of digital technologies.

Based on these criticalities, the main issue is how to achieve sustainability in a system characterized by growing demand and limited resources, and affected by strong fragmentation. Innovation is crucial in healthcare services to improve data flow and focus the process on patients; however, in order to be properly implemented, innovation needs to be pondered from a managerial perspective. Two main issues have to be faced for managing the complexity of the context: overcoming fragmentation and efficiently managing patients' care/flow.

The pandemic emergency and funds invested for facing it accelerated digital transformation and the emergence of innovative business models to accommodate the required changes. Indeed, digital innovation usually refers to technology innovation applied to processes and services, but it also means new business models, such as digital platforms (Liu et al., 2022). Digital innovation means applying digital technology platforms as means or ends to products, processes, or business models innovation within and across organizations (Ciriello et al., 2018). By implementing digital technology, any digital device can store, edit, transmit, and trace information (Kallinikos et al., 2013; Yoo et al., 2010). Moreover, digital innovation boosts a virtuous cycle of innovation: indeed, in order to make the system work, digital technology needs to be supported, in turn, by other digital technologies, encouraging the development of further innovations (De Reuver et al., 2018).

In terms of typologies of innovation in healthcare, they usually are based on breakthrough technology in medical devices, procedures, and treatments; thus, there is a gap in implementing innovation in information technology, networking, and communications. Innovative ways to manage, store, and share patient information need to be considered. ICTs and digital tools enable secure and ubiquitous access of patients to personal data, enabling them to gain control over the information about their health (Hackett et al., 2019).

Innovative healthcare solutions can solve sector fragmentation and overcome silos mentality by improving multidirectional collaboration and communication. Indeed, by adopting an integrated platform shared among healthcare stakeholders, it is possible to decrease the burden from the patients' perspectives by reducing delays, duplications of care, and the necessity to bring paper reports for each visit. In this way, clinicians could easily share information with a centralized system through a unique integrated channel.

Technology can be seen as an active tool embedded into the health system, allowing to customize the clinicians-patients relationship, facilitating remote human touch. Due to the digital divide, the human touch is still considered crucial, especially in the healthcare sector. Indeed, technologies available to patients are very limited in healthcare compared to other sectors. In Italy there is a relevant digital exclusion of people without access to the digital channel due to language or lack of skills. Hence, it is clear that healthcare represents a sector where the human touch is preferred over digitalization. This digital divide has to be considered since, according to the BES 2020 Report, a gap in digital access is evident in terms of gender, territorial gap, and age. All these gaps need to be filled to ensure accessibility and continuity of care to the entire population, both in ordinary and pandemic situations. An effort should be made to improve health literacy by providing transparent information related to prevention, patient safety, outcomes, and patients' feedback. The patients have to be informed in order to improve the level of awareness related to their health, making them autonomous in decision-making, treatments, and comparing alternatives.

Adopting an inclusive approach needs to consider the minorities potentially excluded by digitalization, particularly elderly people, due to the extension of life expectancy and increase in chronic diseases. Therefore, it is possible to reflect on the potential of remote data management for the different types of patients in order to ensure continuity of care for the population. This choice mainly focuses on patients who overcome the emergency and need to receive a cure at home or who are not able to go to the hospital due to critical conditions. However, remote care can also be used for routine visits when they do not require to be performed in person. It means building a new type of relationship in which health service needs to be cocreated between patients, healthcare professionals, and the whole network of stakeholders.

Research on patients' needs is necessary besides the involvement of the other stakeholders to develop and launch new services or improve existing ones. In order to propose technologies for both healthcare professionals and patients, a plan focused on service inclusion is essential. From the patient perspective, it is clear that innovating does not necessarily imply new treatments and medicines but improving quality of life through service innovation by also proposing different solutions, non-pharmaceutical options, or a new way of delivering care. Service innovation is one of the three strategic priorities for service research (Ostrom et al., 2015); thus, a key priority is to broaden the understanding of innovation to shed light on how to implement it in a specific framework.

Service innovation research is characterized by firm centricity and traces innovation in terms of outputs or processes (Helkkula et al., 2018); on the contrary, in the healthcare context, innovation goes beyond firm-centered vision by concentrating on value cocreation and patient centricity (Lusch & Nambisan, 2015; Vargo et al., 2015). This evolution is also reflected in the evolution of innovation archetypes. Past literature divides between the two archetypes of product and process innovation (Abernathy & Townsend, 1975), with innovation research focusing mainly on output and process; thereafter, considering innovation from a value cocreation perspective, the consumer role has switched from being seen as a passive recipient of market offerings (Vargo & Lusch, 2004). Innovation moves toward improving customer value cocreation instead of only proposing a new offering (Rubalcaba et al., 2012), and the perspectives of both firms and customers have been involved in service innovation. By embracing a value cocreation vision, service research has moved toward a more experiential (and systemic) understanding of value creation (Karpen et al., 2012; Prahalad & Ramaswamy, 2003).

These archetypes can be used in characterizing the differing theoretical lenses applied to service innovation (Brodie, 2014; Doty & Glick, 1994; McKelvey, 1975). Helkkula et al. (2018) propose four theoretical archetypes of service innovation: output-based, process-based, experiential, and systemic archetypes. The *output archetypes* mean that value is embedded in the service offering acquired by the consumers (Grönroos & Voima, 2013) regardless of their level of participation. It consists in creating novel outputs with valuable attributes (value-in-exchange). In this scenario, production and consumption are separated, with the firm as an active developer and the consumer as a passive adopter. In healthcare, this type of innovation regards infrastructures or product innovation, such as the introduction of an asset/service that is new or significantly improved compared to its previous characteristics or use. The improvements are related to technical specifications, components and materials, incorporated elements, user friendliness, or other functional characteristics.

The *process archetypes* conceive service innovation as an activity rather than an output (Toivonen & Tuominen, 2009) with the consumer participating in the production process (Grönroos, 1998). It concerns applying new ideas or current applications in different ways throughout the service process (value-in-use). A process-based archetype applies to any change in the service creation process that influences the emergence of value-in-use (Gallouj & Savona, 2009). Some examples of process innovation in healthcare are implementing new or significantly improved production/delivery modes, such as substantial changes in techniques, equipment, and software.

A phenomenological understanding of experience as individual and subjective informs the *experiential archetypes*. Indeed, customer interpretation is fundamental in shaping individual service innovation experience (Husserl, 1970). Hence, the service innovation experience is determined by the beneficiary (Vargo & Lusch, 2008), is subjective, and is influenced by sensemaking and social context (Helkkula & Holopainen, 2011). On this purpose, research on this type of archetype focuses on value and particularly on value cocreation (Helkkula et al., 2012; McColl-Kennedy et al., 2012; Vargo & Lusch, 2008). It concerns cocreating valuable service experiences for all the involved actors (value-in-experience). In healthcare, some examples are innovations aimed at enhancing life expectancy, quality of life, diagnostic, treatment options, care delivery, medications, and surgical interventions, as well as improving the efficiency and cost-effectiveness of the healthcare system (Varkey et al., 2008).

The *systemic* archetypes are informed by a holistic belief that the whole is more than the sum of the parts (Sheth et al., 1988). Focusing the attention on separate specific parts is not efficient; thus, the unit of analysis for service innovation research is more comprehensive, considering the service ecosystem and going beyond the specific service offering (Rubalcaba et al., 2012). This archetype of service innovation focuses on resource integration among various actors existing in a context: firms cannot design or create market offerings without connecting and integrating resources (value-in-context) with multiple actors in the network (Helkkula et al., 2018). The systemic archetype can be represented by structural innovation, which creates new business models and affects internal and external infrastructures. In this case, healthcare innovation could concern, for instance, the possibility to share in real-time information among clinicians and colleagues in the same department/hospital or across healthcare organizations at the country level. This type of innovation could also impact patients by allowing them to access their records and transmit them to clinicians.

This scenario represents the future Smart healthcare, which incorporates digital technologies to quickly and easily navigate health information, linking individuals, resources, and organizations, and then promptly react to health demands and challenges (Muhammad et al., 2021). Smart healthcare links different stakeholders in the health system, such as patients, healthcare professionals, organizations, and regulators. This network is enabled by emerging technologies, including artificial intelligence (AI), internet of things (IoT), cloud computing, blockchain, sensors, and 5G technology that continue to evolve (Mbunge, 2020). These technologies play an essential role in developing the emerging innovative scenario of Healthcare 5.0.

Implementing a hybrid healthcare delivery model based on digitization and human touch requires several factors (Ciasullo et al., 2021). Patients' needs and the related evolution should be monitored throughout the healthcare experience (Rubenstein et al., 2014; Cook et al., 2015). Technologies such as ICTs and digital tools should be integrated into healthcare delivery with the aim to: enable a continuous exchange among patients and healthcare professionals (Robben et al., 2012); coach patients, allowing them to fully recognize their healthcare needs and be actively engaged in health promotion and risk prevention initiatives (Graffigna et al., 2014); entitle patients with greater control over resources available for wellbeing improvement (Gammon et al., 2014). A transition toward personalized care, where engaged patients play the active role of healthcare service prosumers (Fontaine et al., 2015), requires change management that jointly leverages the transformation of organizational cultures, the reconfiguration of healthcare delivery systems, and digitization (Ciasullo et al., 2021).

2.1   The Era of Smart Healthcare

A paradigm shift in digital technologies, from traditional healthcare to Smart healthcare, is set to revolutionize healthcare systems globally (Mbunge et al., 2021).

Through digitization and the influence of Industry 4.0, healthcare practitioners are encouraged to collect patient concerns and carefully identify solutions to ensure a positive patient experience (Mukherjee & Singh, 2020).

By retracing healthcare evolution so far, several phases have been identified that have been summarized in Fig. 2.1.

- The era of Healthcare 1.0: healthcare systems mainly based on paper-based systems due to the lack of digital technologies (Chanchaichujit et al., 2019). Patients and healthcare professionals, through consultation, testing, and diagnosis, capture health data and medical prescriptions on paper manually (Li & Carayon, 2021). This model has been prevalent in healthcare practice for many years (Bhavin et al., 2021). The main issues were related to patients' records lost, deterioration, and privacy.
- The era of Healthcare 2.0 (e-Health): aims at reinforcing the privacy and security of health records while improving maintenance and scalability (Bhavin et al., 2021). The genesis of digital technology transformed several health systems and improved efficiency in data capturing, accessibility, and sharing (Bhattacharya et al., 2019). In this generation, new advanced medical devices and equipment were developed along with significant developments in the manufacturing industry. Digital imaging test equipment, digital tracking devices, surgical tools, and life support equipment were developed in Healthcare 2.0 (Li & Carayon, 2021).

- The era of Healthcare 3.0: technological advancements in the medical field, telehealth, and electronic health records were added to Healthcare 2.0 (Kumari et al., 2018). Electronic health records help healthcare professionals to upload, share, and access health data on the cloud anytime. The main threats are related to security attacks to patients' critical data.
- The era of Healthcare 4.0: to alleviate the above challenge, new technologies (i.e., AI, IoT, mobile technologies, blockchain, virtual reality, big data, etc.) have been added to Healthcare 3.0. The ultimate goal of Healthcare 4.0 is to provide patient-centric healthcare services through smart care, connected care, and personalized medicine (Li & Carayon, 2021). Healthcare 4.0 incorporates the principles and applications of Industry 4.0 into healthcare, enabling real-time customization of care to patients and professionals; it promotes communication between actors in the healthcare value chain and dissemination of health-related information; it collects data on processes, patients, equipment, and materials; it handles and transforms health data into information and digitalizes healthcare processes. New technological tools support resilient performance in healthcare systems and the capacity of adaptation to complex environments.

Health 4.0 is defined as a shift from mass and reactive healthcare to personalized and proactive healthcare (El Saddik et al., 2019). Health 4.0 is composed of interoperability, virtualization, decentralization, real-time capability, service orientation, and modularity, and it represents a process of virtualization in order to enable real-time personalization of health and care for patients, healthcare professionals, and carers (Thuemmler & Bai, 2017; Hermann et al., 2016). This scenario is feasible through data acquisition, network generation, interconnections, data collection and processing, and assisted diagnosis. Different sources (i.e., smart implants and sensors) and computer networks manage patients' data in an integrated way. Heterogeneous data are processed through advanced techniques (Loeza-Mejía et al., 2021). Finally, the assisted diagnosis is carried out by artificial intelligence techniques, machine learning, and deep learning, whereas the assisted treatment is carried out through telesurgery, robotic surgery, and augmented reality. The Fig. 2.2 illustrates the integration among Healthcare 4.0 technologies.

In Healthcare 4.0, different technologies coexist and enable each other to function. All these technologies contribute to making the system work

HEALTHCARE 1.0	HEALTHCARE 3.0
• Paper-based systems • Health data and medical prescriptions captured on the paper manually • Output archetypes • Type of innovation: Product innovation Examples: new goods or improvements in technical specifications, components and materials or other functional characteristics	• Digitization • Uploading, sharing, and accessing health data on the cloud anytime • Process archetypes • Type of innovation: Process innovation Examples: telehealth and electronic health records
HEALTHCARE 2.0	**HEALTHCARE 4.0**
• Digitization • Data capturing, accessibility, and sharing through digital technologies • Output archetypes • Type of innovation: Product innovation Examples: new advanced medical devices and equipment, developments in the manufacturing industry	• Digitization • Patient-centric healthcare services through smart care, connected care, and real-time personalized care • Tools for communication between actors, dissemination of health-related information, tool for collecting, processing and transforming health data into information; • infrastructures for digitization and automation of healthcare processes. • Experiential and systemic archetypes • Type of innovation: structural innovation Examples: Cyber-Physical Systems, Internet of Things, Virtual reality, Cloud Computing, Big Data Analytics, Blockchain

Fig. 2.1 Healthcare evolution

in each step, from data acquisition to assisted diagnosis or treatment. Healthcare 4.0 solutions support clinicians in decision-making, providing treatments in a less invasive and more interactive way and improving diagnosis and rehabilitation treatments (Loeza-Mejía et al., 2021).

From the patients' perspective, new technologies can also be used to improve the level of awareness related to health: this is the case of the application of gamification, which consists in applying game mechanics to non-game contexts (Deterding et al., 2011). It is a promising tool for improving learning outcomes by strengthening learning behaviors and attitudes toward learning (van Gaalen et al., 2021). Moreover, it involves users in raising awareness and being involved in their health conditions (Ramdhani et al., 2021).

Digital expansion and innovative medical technologies have led to the development of advanced medical and tracking systems typical of Healthcare 4.0. The trend is to transform healthcare systems toward a value-based system to improve patient-centric services through smart care, connected care, and personalized medicine (Kumari et al., 2018). The further evolution of Healthcare 4.0 toward Healthcare 5.0 is foreseen to

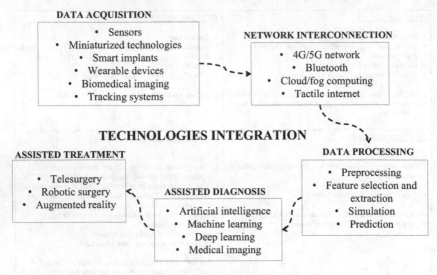

Fig. 2.2 Healthcare 4.0 technologies integration

continuously redefine how modern digital high-tech companies improve business operations and increase efficiency across the value chain (Mbunge et al., 2021).

Digitization is a lever to activate the transformative process aimed at overcoming the main healthcare gaps enabling value cocreation and patient centricity. The scope is to overcome the silos mentality and fragmentation through digital solutions and integrated digital pathway infrastructures that support the patients in selecting reliable sources of information, sharing data, and interacting with clinicians. In order to follow this strategy, patients and healthcare professionals should be included in the healthcare system as partners and adequately trained, implying also a change of behavior. Indeed, in addition to this culture shift, all stakeholders need to adapt to new environments, technologies, and regulations (Bause et al., 2019).

REFERENCES

Abernathy, W. J., & Townsend, P. L. (1975). Technology, productivity and process change. *Technological Forecasting and Social Change, 7*(4), 379–396.

Bause, M., Esfahani, B. K., Forbes, H., & Schaefer, D. (2019). Design for health 4.0: Exploration of a new area. In *Proceedings of the design society: International conference on engineering design* (Vol. 1, No. 1, pp. 887–896). Cambridge University Press.

Bhattacharya, P., Tanwar, S., Bodkhe, U., Tyagi, S., & Kumar, N. (2019). Bindaas: Blockchain-based deep-learning as-a-service in healthcare 4.0 applications. *IEEE Transactions on Network Science and Engineering, 8*(2), 1242–1255.

Bhavin, M., Tanwar, S., Sharma, N., Tyagi, S., & Kumar, N. (2021). Blockchain and quantum blind signature-based hybrid scheme for healthcare 5.0 applications. *Journal of Information Security and Applications, 56*, 102673.

Brodie, R. J. (2014). Future of theorizing in marketing: Increasing contribution by bridging theory and practice. In *The Routledge companion to the future of marketing* (pp. 123–139). Routledge.

Chanchaichujit, J., Tan, A., Meng, F., & Eaimkhong, S. (2019). An introduction to healthcare 4.0. In *Healthcare 4.0* (pp. 1–15). Palgrave Pivot.

Ciasullo, M. V., Carli, M., Lim, W. M., & Palumbo, R. (2021). An open innovation approach to co-produce scientific knowledge: An examination of citizen science in the healthcare ecosystem. *European Journal of Innovation Management, 25*(6), 365–392.

Ciriello, R. F., Richter, A., & Schwabe, G. (2018). Digital innovation. *Business & Information Systems Engineering, 60*(6), 563–569.

Cook, N., Hollar, L., Isaac, E., Paul, L., Amofah, A., & Shi, L. (2015). Patient experience in health center medical homes. *Journal of Community Health, 40*(6), 1155–1164.

De Reuver, M., Sørensen, C., & Basole, R. C. (2018). The digital platform: A research agenda. *Journal of Information Technology, 33*(2), 124–135.

Deterding, S., Dixon, D., Khaled, R., & Nacke, L. (2011, September). From game design elements to gamefulness: defining" gamification". In Proceedings of the 15th international academic MindTrek conference: Envisioning future media environments (pp. 9–15).

Doty, D. H., & Glick, W. H. (1994). Typologies as a unique form of theory building: Toward improved understanding and modeling. *Academy of Management Review, 19*(2), 230–251.

El Saddik, A., Hossain, M. S., & Kantarci, B. (2019). *Connected health in smart cities*. Springer Nature.

Fontaine, P., Whitebird, R., Solberg, L. I., Tillema, J., Smithson, A., & Crabtree, B. F. (2015). Minnesota's early experience with medical home implementation: Viewpoints from the front lines. *Journal of General Internal Medicine, 30*(7), 899–906.

Gallouj, F., & Savona, M. (2009). Innovation in services: A review of the debate and a research agenda. *Journal of Evolutionary Economics, 19*(2), 149–172.

Gammon, D., Strand, M., & Eng, L. S. (2014). Service users' perspectives in the design of an online tool for assisted self-help in mental health: A case study of implications. *International Journal of Mental Health Systems, 8*(1), 1–8.

Graffigna, G., Barello, S., Triberti, S., Wiederhold, B. K., Bosio, A. C., & Riva, G. (2014). Enabling eHealth as a pathway for patient engagement: A toolkit for medical practice. *Studies in Health Technology and Informatics, 199,* 13–21.

Grönroos, C. (1998). Marketing services: The case of a missing product. *Journal of Business & Industrial Marketing, 13,* 322–338.

Grönroos, C., & Voima, P. (2013). Critical service logic: Making sense of value creation and co-creation. *Journal of the Academy of Marketing Science, 41*(2), 133–150.

Hackett, C., Brennan, K., Fowler, H. S., & Leaver, C. (2019). Valuing citizen access to digital health services: Applied value-based outcomes in the Canadian context and tools for modernizing health systems. *Journal of Medical Internet Research, 21*(6), 151–164.

Helkkula, A., & Holopainen, M. (2011). Service innovation as an experience: Differences between employee and user narratives. In *User-based innovation in services*. Edward Elgar Publishing.

Helkkula, A., Kelleher, C., & Pihlström, M. (2012). Characterizing value as an experience: Implications for service researchers and managers. *Journal of Service Research, 15*(1), 59–75.

Helkkula, A., Kowalkowski, C., & Tronvoll, B. (2018). Archetypes of service innovation: Implications for value cocreation. *Journal of Service Research, 21*(3), 284–301.

Hermann, M., Pentek, T., & Otto, B. (2016). Design principles for Industrie 4.0 scenarios. In *2016 49th Hawaii international conference on system sciences (HICSS)* (pp. 3928–3937). IEEE.

Husserl, E. (1970). *The crisis of European sciences and transcendental phenomenology: An introduction to phenomenological philosophy*. Northwestern University Press.

Kallinikos, J., Aaltonen, A., & Marton, A. (2013). The ambivalent ontology of digital artifacts. *MIS Quarterly, 37,* 357–370.

Karpen, I. O., Bove, L. L., & Lukas, B. A. (2012). Linking service-dominant logic and strategic business practice: A conceptual model of a service-dominant orientation. *Journal of Service Research, 15*(1), 21–38.

Kumari, A., Tanwar, S., Tyagi, S., & Kumar, N. (2018). Fog computing for Healthcare 4.0 environment: Opportunities and challenges. *Computers & Electrical Engineering, 72,* 1–13.

Li, J., & Carayon, P. (2021). Health Care 4.0: A vision for smart and connected health care. *IISE Transactions on Healthcare Systems Engineering, 11*(3), 171–180.

Liu, Z., Shi, Y., & Yang, B. (2022). Open innovation in times of crisis: An overview of the healthcare sector in response to the COVID-19 pandemic. *Journal of Open Innovation: Technology, Market, and Complexity, 8*(1), 21.

Loeza-Mejía, C. I., Sánchez-DelaCruz, E., Pozos-Parra, P., & Landero-Hernández, L. A. (2021). The potential and challenges of Health 4.0 to face COVID-19 pandemic: A rapid review. *Health and Technology, 11*(6), 1321–1330.

Lusch, R. F., & Nambisan, S. (2015). Service innovation. *MIS Quarterly, 39*(1), 155–176.

Mbunge, E. (2020). Integrating emerging technologies into COVID-19 contact tracing: Opportunities, challenges and pitfalls. *Diabetes & Metabolic Syndrome: Clinical Research & Reviews, 14*(6), 1631–1636.

Mbunge, E., Muchemwa, B., & Batani, J. (2021). Sensors and healthcare 5.0: transformative shift in virtual care through emerging digital health technologies. *Global Health Journal, 5*(4), 169–177.

McColl-Kennedy, J. R., Vargo, S. L., Dagger, T. S., Sweeney, J. C., & Kasteren, Y. V. (2012). Health care customer value cocreation practice styles. *Journal of Service Research, 15*(4), 370–389.

McKelvey, B. (1975). Guidelines for the empirical classification of organizations. *Administrative Science Quarterly, 20*, 509–525.

Muhammad, G., Alshehri, F., Karray, F., El Saddik, A., Alsulaiman, M., & Falk, T. H. (2021). A comprehensive survey on multimodal medical signals fusion for smart healthcare systems. *Information Fusion, 76*, 355–375.

Mukherjee, P., & Singh, D. (2020). The opportunities of blockchain in health 4.0. In *Blockchain technology for industry 4.0* (pp. 149–164). Springer.

Ostrom, A. L., Parasuraman, A., Bowen, D. E., Patrício, L., & Voss, C. A. (2015). Service research priorities in a rapidly changing context. *Journal of Service Research, 18*(2), 127–159.

Prahalad, C. K., & Ramaswamy, V. (2003). The new frontier of experience innovation. *MIT Sloan Management Review, 44*(4), 12.

Ramdhani, R. M., Nurrahman, A. D., Affendi, P. H., Hasugian, L. P., & Rafdhi, A. A. (2021). Gamification implementation in health service website in 5.0 society era. *International Journal of Research and Applied Technology, 1*(2), 424–430.

Robben, S., Perry, M., van Nieuwenhuijzen, L., van Achterberg, T., Rikkert, M. O., Schers, H., et al. (2012). Impact of interprofessional education on collaboration attitudes, skills, and behavior among primary care professionals. *Journal of Continuing Education in the Health Professions, 32*(3), 196–204.

Rubalcaba, L., Michel, S., Sundbo, J., Brown, S. W., & Reynoso, J. (2012). Shaping, organizing, and rethinking service innovation: A multidimensional framework. *Journal of Service Management, 23*(5), 696–715.

Rubenstein, L. V., Stockdale, S. E., Sapir, N., Altman, L., Dresselhaus, T., Salem-Schatz, S., Vivell, S., Ovretveit, J., Hamilton, A. B., & Yano, E. M. (2014). A patient-centered primary care practice approach using evidence-based quality improvement: Rationale, methods, and early assessment of implementation. *Journal of General Internal Medicine, 29*(2), 589–597.

Sheth, J. N., Gardner, D. M., & Garrett, D. E. (1988). *Marketing theory: Evolution and evaluation* (Vol. 12). Wiley.

Thuemmler, C., & Bai, C. (2017). Health 4.0: Application of industry 4.0 design principles in future asthma management. In *Health 4.0: How virtualization and big data are revolutionizing healthcare* (pp. 23–37). Springer.

Toivonen, M., & Tuominen, T. (2009). Emergence of innovations in services. *The Service Industries Journal, 29*(7), 887–902.

van Gaalen, A. E., Brouwer, J., Schönrock-Adema, J., Bouwkamp-Timmer, T., Jaarsma, A. D. C., & Georgiadis, J. R. (2021). Gamification of health professions education: A systematic review. *Advances in Health Sciences Education, 26*(2), 683–711.

Vargo, S. L., & Lusch, R. F. (2004). The four service marketing myths: Remnants of a goods-based, manufacturing model. *Journal of Service Research, 6*(4), 324–335.

Vargo, S. L., & Lusch, R. F. (2008). Service-dominant logic: Continuing the evolution. *Journal of the Academy of Marketing Science, 36*(1), 1–10.

Vargo, S. L., Wieland, H., & Akaka, M. A. (2015). Innovation through institutionalization: A service ecosystems perspective. *Industrial Marketing Management, 44*, 63–72.

Varkey, P., Horne, A., & Bennet, K. E. (2008). Innovation in health care: A primer. *American Journal of Medical Quality, 23*(5), 382–388.

Yoo, Y., Henfridsson, O., & Lyytinen, K. (2010). Research commentary—The new organizing logic of digital innovation: An agenda for information systems research. *Information Systems Research, 21*(4), 724–735.

CHAPTER 3

One Digital Health

Abstract The introduction of the One Health (OH) concept has represented a decisive moment. This approach has been at first applied to the animal context for being expanded later on toward a holistic approach to sustainable development in which the relationship between humans, animals, and the environment becomes inextricably linked and requires a global approach and effort.

This approach requires a collaborative effort of multiple disciplines to contribute toward health for people, animals, and the environment. Advances in digital technology introduce One Digital Health (ODH) concept which analyzes the digital health ecosystem components and how technologies can support healthcare and wellbeing. ODH process involves integrating human and veterinary medical data into real-time information systems to support public health in facing emerging challenges due to the growing overlap between human and animal habitats. With OH and ODH the concept of human health is integrated with wellbeing and sustainability.

Keywords One Health • One Digital Health • Sustainability • Digitization

M. Toni, G. Mattia, *The Digital Healthcare Revolution*,
https://doi.org/10.1007/978-3-031-16340-1_3

3.1   One Health

The relationships between humans, animals, and the environment are crucial for the survival of all species and our planet (Amuasi et al., 2020). Industrialization and urbanization have advanced human health in considerable ways, even though this evolution exposes humans to global health risks (Klohe et al., 2019). These challenges, such as emerging infectious diseases, are further impacted by climate change, deforestation, poverty, health disparities, unsustainable population growth, conflict, and migration (Ogunseitan, 2022).

The majority of emergent infectious diseases originate in animals, especially wildlife (Taylor et al., 2001), and in many cases, they are consequences of human activities, for instance, land use, urbanization, agriculture intensification, and international travel and trade (Mackenzie & Jeggo, 2019; Jones et al., 2008).

Human population health and existence need to be redefined considering increasing current challenges and the complex interconnectedness of all living species and the environment (Zinsstag et al., 2015; Gronvall et al., 2014; Amuasi et al., 2020). Health problems need to be managed through a collaborative and multidisciplinary approach, cutting across boundaries of health disciplines (animal, human, and environmental health) in order to undertake a risk assessment and a monitoring plan (Mackenzie & Jeggo, 2019).

One Health (OH) approach highlights the concurrent benefits of overcoming disciplinary silos to cooperate between different health sciences, including human, animal, and environmental perspectives (Min et al., 2013). All science fields are strongly interconnected and interdependent.

The term OH first emerged at the global level as an approach to address interactions between animals and humans and its association with emerging severe acute zoonotic diseases (Mackenzie & Jeggo, 2019; Min et al., 2013). The concept of OH dates back, starting with the term zoonosis coined by Rudolf Virchow to define the transmission of infectious diseases from animals to humans. Thereafter, Schwabe (1984) introduces the concept of One Medicine, reinforcing the importance of human and veterinary medicine collaboration.

The evolution of One Medicine concept is OH, and its modern origins are attributed to the 12 Manhattan Principles, which propose an international, interdisciplinary approach to prevent diseases (Mackenzie & Jeggo, 2019), specifically animal-human transmissible and communicable diseases. The "Manhattan Principles" are a series of strategic goals, adopting a cross-disciplinary approach that recognizes a link between human and animal health with diseases impacting further contexts, such as food supplies and economies. Wildlife health has become essential to global disease prevention, surveillance, control, and mitigation (Wildlife Conservation Society, 2004; Mackenzie & Jeggo, 2019).

OH has been established on two fundamental arguments: the inextricable link between humans, animals, and their shared environment (Conrad et al., 2009, Min et al., 2013; Mackenzie & Jeggo, 2019); and, then, the contribution toward health for people, animals, and the environment through a multiple disciplines collaborative effort.

In terms of definition, "Health" is defined by the World Health Organization (WHO) as a state of complete physical, mental, and social wellbeing (WHO, 1948). The concept of OH has been defined in several ways. The WHO currently defines it as an approach in which different sectors collaborate to achieve better public health outcomes by implementing programs, research, policy, and legislation (Ogunseitan, 2022).

In order to define the dimensions of OH, the Lancet One Health Commission identifies three distinct but interrelated dimensions that are examined in relation to infectious diseases, non-communicable diseases, and antimicrobial resistance (AMR) (Amuasi et al., 2020). The first dimension is related to shared environment, considering how animals (including livestock, companions, and wildlife) share a common environment with humans in rural and urban settings. The second dimension regards safe food and food systems, in which the relationship between humans and animals is clear since people rely on animals both as food and to help produce food. Food safety and security need to be explored using innovative research methods (Grace, 2015, Thanner et al., 2016). The third dimension concerns the shared medicines and interventions since several drugs used to treat human health conditions originated from animal agriculture (Callaway & Cyranoski, 2015).

Operationalizing OH requires integrating animal and human health systems, and digitization can be a support for surveillance, big data exploitation related to animals, humans, and plants, and digital health implementation.

3.2   ONE HEALTH AND SUSTAINABILITY

The WHO has linked OH to Sustainable Development Goals (SDG) (Gostin & Friedman, 2015) and particularly to the targets related to ensuring good health and wellbeing for all at all ages (SDG-3). Moreover, it also refers to nutrition (SDG-2) because it is strongly linked to ecosystem health, animal health, wildlife diversity, and population distribution (Osterhaus et al., 2020); thus, it is important to manage environmental degradation and biodiversity loss.

In this context, OH and sustainability science have a common scope that deals with inequalities in healthcare access and social support systems, reducing the impacts of risk factors (i.e., disease, natural disaster, and climate change) on the population (Ogunseitan, 2022). Focusing on consequences, responses, and actions at the animal-human-ecosystems level (Mackenzie & Jeggo, 2019), the OH concept examines emerging and endemic zoonoses and disease, antimicrobial resistance, and food safety. The Sustainable Development Goals are embedded into the OH strategy for healthy people living on a habitable planet (Amuasi et al., 2020; Gostin & Friedman, 2015).

OH comprises the assessment and monitoring of the environmental impacts and the potential risks on healthcare systems, public health, biodiversity, and food security due to the interconnections between humans, animals, and environment (Zinsstag et al., 2011; Rosa, 2017; Osterhaus, 2019; Ashleigh, 2019). For this reason, OH concept is often framed as a pathway to sustainability because it links biodiversity, particularly regarding wildlife and agricultural animals, to human health, with the environment playing an intermediary role (Coker et al., 2011; Lebov et al., 2017; Xie et al., 2017; Valeix, 2018; Destoumieux-Garzón et al., 2018; van Herten et al., 2019).

The agenda for OH implementation science is urgent, and it is also linked to the strategic management of cities and ecosystem services in which people could at any time come under quarantine due to infectious diseases (Ogunseitan, 2022). Therefore, OH research requires close collaboration among health practitioners, public health workers, biologists, and environmental science specialists. This theme is particularly relevant in order to be able to respond to natural disasters and climate change that simultaneously involve habitats of humans, animals, and plants. OH promotes original thinking and generates solutions by embracing other disciplines and domains to the complex global health challenges of modern times, providing an approach for exploiting this knowledge to ensure a healthy future for people, animals, and the planet (Amuasi et al., 2020).

Interconnections between people's health and nature and the interrelation of health system with others (i.e., the economic one) are widely acknowledged; this implies a switch from egocentric to ecocentric vision. The egocentric paradigm is grounded on the assumption that what is suitable for the individual is good also for society; whereas, in the ecocentric paradigm, there is a broader perspective in which the focus is on the environment considered whole and interconnected (Kleffel, 1996). Hence, the ecocentric paradigm has a broader view of sustainability, considering the entire network of connected, interdependent organisms that exchange resources from each other in a specific environment.

3.3   ONE DIGITAL HEALTH

The evolution of digital technology has resulted in evidence-based, accessible information that is able to enhance public health efficacy and scientific knowledge development. Integrating digital technologies even outside the medical context along with citizens' active engagement generates considerable volumes of real-time data through different systems, enhancing population health, efficiency, precision, and personalization in healthcare delivery. As a consequence, advances in digital technology introduce One Digital Health (ODH) concept (Benis et al., 2021). This framework integrates perspectives of health informatics and digital health (Lovis, 2017) with OH (Mackenzie & Jeggo, 2019) and environmental research. The focus is to analyze the digital health ecosystem components and how technologies may support healthcare and wellbeing. ODH aims to digitally transform future health ecosystems by implementing a systemic approach supported by technologies to study the interconnections between human health, animal health, and the surrounding environment (Benis et al., 2021). In order to integrate and use the information generated by the ODH, data should be findable, accessible, interoperable, and reusable (Wilkinson et al., 2018, Benis & Tamburis, 2021). In this way, people would be able to digitally engage with their own health and wellbeing through health prevention activities, self-management, and control.

In terms of composition, ODH has a unified structure identified through the One Digital Health Steering Wheel: it comprises three intertwined levels (key dimensions, perspectives, and dimensions) wherein digital technology represents a determining factor (Benis et al., 2021).

The two key dimensions are digital health and One Health. Digitization of health services (see Chap. 2) has brought to digital health (Ahmadvand et al., 2019), which serves different purposes: ubiquitously collecting and storing data, information, and knowledge to deliver healthcare and preventive activities efficiently; health and treatments customization; health promotion, wellbeing, and efficient self-management. The digitalized data are related to the digital transformation of human and animal health data and digital nature conservation in biodiversity and wildlife conservation, food security, antimicrobial resistance, and climate change. These data can be collected through technologies such as smart devices, connected medical equipment, or connected wellness equipment and exploiting IOT, artificial intelligence, big data, and robotics (Chute & French, 2019). Implementing these technologies in everyday life allows surveillance, contact tracing, testing, confinement, and other health and care interventions (Whitelaw et al., 2020). This process involves integrating human and veterinary medical data into real-time information systems that support public health (Leroy et al., 2020).

Besides the two key dimensions, the three ODH perspectives are individual health and wellbeing, population and society, and ecosystem.

The first perspective is based on the awareness of shared risks among animal and human populations. A transformative approach is aimed at reinforcing traditional surveillance systems' ability to prevent and control diseases and at linking intersectoral health data through accurate and preventive methods and innovative managing tools (Rosa, 2017, Asokan & Asokan, 2015, Ji et al., 2015) besides innovative ways for managing data (big data and smart data).

The second perspective is related to the broader view of population and society to understand the differences and variability between individuals to provide personalized health (i.e., genes, environments, digital health literacy, preferences, and lifestyles). Knowledge integration of healthcare, veterinary care, agriculture, meteorology, climate change, environmental protection, and intelligence (Lai et al., 2020) supports the decision-making processes.

The third perspective is related to the whole ecosystem, including all living and nonliving species. It observes the interaction between population and ecosystem, referring to biodiversity conservation and the links among the healthcare and wellbeing of all components (Rook, 2013).

The implementation of these perspectives is possible through adequate data collection tools (collecting, digitalizing, and assembling data also through geolocalization), accessible data management based on environmental management and monitoring information systems, and decision support algorithms (Karatzas, 2011; Khaiter & Erechtchoukova, 2020).

The last layer is composed of five dimensions: Education (health and digitalization learning opportunities to citizens), Citizen's Engagement Supporting (supporting digital health literacy by actively encouraging everyone to engage with health), Human and Veterinary Healthcare (digitization enables preventive recommendations and predictive alert systems for integrated personalized care), Healthcare Industry 4.0 (enhancing the automation and connectivity of systems, by increasing the interoperability and flexibility of systems and allowing for decentralized, real-time data collection and storage), and Environment (integrated into healthcare management systems, to enrich data, information, and knowledge about environmental exposures and health risks).

ODH implementation is enabled by digital technologies and collaboration among practitioners in OH and digital health communities. This coordinated effort allows observing how humans and animals' activities affect each other's health and managing these complex interactions in relation to their ecosystems. There is a need for initiatives and actions to dissolve the research silos among disciplines through ad hoc infrastructures and complementary knowledge. Digitization supports OH and ODH through digital functionalities (Rüegg et al., 2018) that collect data on outcomes and effects to address systems' challenges (Rock et al., 2009). OH becomes particularly relevant due to the population growth that will lead human and animal habitats overlapping, with the consequent exposure to potential diseases. Hence, preventive actions are also necessary in other sectors linked to healthcare for protecting food and water from contamination and natural disasters.

References

Ahmadvand, A., Kavanagh, D., Clark, M., Drennan, J., & Nissen, L. (2019). Trends and visibility of "digital health" as a keyword in articles by JMIR publications in the new millennium: Bibliographic-bibliometric analysis. *Journal of Medical Internet Research, 21*(12), e10477.

Amuasi, J. H., Lucas, T., Horton, R., & Winkler, A. S. (2020). Reconnecting for our future: The lancet one health commission. *The Lancet, 395*(10235), 1469–1471.

Ashleigh, C. (2019). Visualising one health. In *One planet, one health*. Sydney University Press.

Asokan, G. V., & Asokan, V. (2015). Leveraging "big data" to enhance the effectiveness of "one health" in an era of health informatics. *Journal of Epidemiology and Global Health, 5*(4), 311–314.

Benis, A., & Tamburis, O. (2021). One Digital Health is FAIR I. In *Applying the FAIR principles to accelerate health research in Europe in the post COVID-19 era: Proceedings of the 2021 EFMI special topic conference* (pp. 287, 57). IOS Press.

Benis, A., Tamburis, O., Chronaki, C., & Moen, A. (2021). One digital health: A unified framework for future health ecosystems. *Journal of Medical Internet Research, 23*(2), e22189.

Callaway, E., & Cyranoski, D. (2015). Anti-parasite drugs sweep Nobel prize in medicine 2015. *Nature, 526*(7572), 174–175.

Chute, C., & French, T. (2019). Introducing care 4.0: An integrated care paradigm built on industry 4.0 capabilities. *International Journal of Environmental Research and Public Health, 16*(12), 2247.

Coker, R., Rushton, J., Mounier-Jack, S., Karimuribo, E., Lutumba, P., Kambarage, D., et al. (2011). Towards a conceptual framework to support one-health research for policy on emerging zoonoses. *The Lancet Infectious Diseases, 11*(4), 326–331.

Conrad, P. A., Mazet, J. A., Clifford, D., Scott, C., & Wilkes, M. (2009). Evolution of a transdisciplinary "One Medicine–One Health" approach to global health education at the University of California, Davis. *Preventive Veterinary Medicine, 92*(4), 268–274.

Destoumieux-Garzón, D., Mavingui, P., Boetsch, G., Boissier, J., Darriet, F., Duboz, P., et al. (2018). The one health concept: 10 years old and a long road ahead. *Frontiers in Veterinary Science, 5*, 14.

Gostin, L. O., & Friedman, E. A. (2015). The sustainable development goals: One-health in the world's development agenda. *JAMA, 314*(24), 2621–2622.

Grace, D. (2015). Review of evidence on antimicrobial resistance and animal agriculture in developing countries. International LivestockResearch Institute(ILRI), https://doi.org/10.12774/eod_cr.june2015.graced.

Gronvall, G., Boddie, C., Knutsson, R., & Colby, M. (2014). One health security: An important component of the global health security agenda. *Biosecurity and Bioterrorism: Biodefense Strategy, Practice, and Science, 12*(5), 221–224.

Ji, X., Cappellari, P., Chun, S., & Geller, J. (2015). Leveraging social data for health care behavior analytics. In *International conference on web engineering* (pp. 667–670). Springer.

Jones, K. E., Patel, N. G., Levy, M. A., Storeygard, A., Balk, D., Gittleman, J. L., & Daszak, P. (2008). Global trends in emerging infectious diseases. *Nature, 451*(7181), 990–993.

Karatzas, K. D. (2011). Participatory environmental sensing for quality of life information services. In *Information technologies in environmental engineering* (pp. 123–133). Springer.

Khaiter, P. A., & Erechtchoukova, M. G. (2020). *Sustainability perspectives: Science, policy and practice.* Springer.

Kleffel, D. (1996). Environmental paradigms: Moving toward an ecocentric perspective. *Advances in Nursing Science, 18*(4), 1–10.

Klohe, K., Amuasi, J., Kaducu, J. M., Haavardsson, I., Bogatyreva, E., Onarheim, K. H., et al. (2019). The 2017 Oslo conference report on neglected tropical diseases and emerging/re-emerging infectious diseases–focus on populations underserved. *Infectious Diseases of Poverty, 8*(1), 1–10.

Lai, Y., Yeung, W., & Celi, L. A. (2020). Urban intelligence for pandemic response. *JMIR Public Health and Surveillance, 6*(2), e18873.

Lebov, J., Grieger, K., Womack, D., Zaccaro, D., Whitehead, N., Kowalcyk, B., & MacDonald, P. D. (2017). A framework for One Health research. *One Health, 3,* 44–50.

Leroy, E. M., Gouilh, M. A., & Brugère-Picoux, J. (2020). The risk of SARS-CoV-2 transmission to pets and other wild and domestic animals strongly mandates a one-health strategy to control the COVID-19 pandemic. *One Health, 10,* 100133.

Lovis, C. (2017). Digital health: A science at crossroads. *International Journal of Medical Informatics, 110,* 108–110.

Mackenzie, J. S., & Jeggo, M. (2019). The One Health approach—Why is it so important? *Tropical Medicine and Infectious Disease, 4*(2), 88.

Min, B., Allen-Scott, L. K., & Buntain, B. (2013). Transdisciplinary research for complex One Health issues: A scoping review of key concepts. *Preventive Veterinary Medicine, 112*(3–4), 222–229.

Ogunseitan, O. A. (2022). One health and the environment: From conceptual framework to implementation science. *Environment: Science and Policy for Sustainable Development, 64*(2), 11–21.

Osterhaus, A. (2019). Welcome to One Health Outlook. *One Health Outlook, 1*(1), 1–2.

Osterhaus, A. D., Vanlangendonck, C., Barbeschi, M., Bruschke, C. J., Christensen, R., Daszak, P., et al. (2020). Make science evolve into a One Health approach to improve health and security: A white paper. *One Health Outlook, 2*(1), 1–32.

Rock, M., Buntain, B. J., Hatfield, J. M., & Hallgrímsson, B. (2009). Animal–human connections, "one health," and the syndemic approach to prevention. *Social Science & Medicine, 68*(6), 991–995.

Rook, G. A. (2013). Regulation of the immune system by biodiversity from the natural environment: An ecosystem service essential to health. *Proceedings of the National Academy of Sciences, 110*(46), 18360–18367.

Rosa, W. (2017). One mind, one health, one planet–a pledge to planetary citizenship. *A new era in global health: Nursing and the United Nations, 2030* (pp. 517–520). Springer.

Rüegg, S. R., Nielsen, L. R., Buttigieg, S. C., Santa, M., Aragrande, M., Canali, M., et al. (2018). A systems approach to evaluate One Health initiatives. *Frontiers in Veterinary Science, 5*, 23.

Schwabe, C. (1984). *Veterinary medicine and human health.* Williams & Wilkins.

Taylor, L. H., Latham, S. M., & Woolhouse, M. E. (2001). Risk factors for human disease emergence. *Philosophical Transactions of the Royal Society of London. Series B: Biological Sciences, 356*(1411), 983–989.

Thanner, S., Drissner, D., & Walsh, F. (2016). Antimicrobial resistance in agriculture. *mBio, 7*(2), e02227–e02215.

Valeix, S. F. (2018). One health integration: A proposed framework for a study on veterinarians and zoonotic disease management in Ghana. *Frontiers in Veterinary Science, 5*, 85.

van Herten, J., Bovenkerk, B., & Verweij, M. (2019). One Health as a moral dilemma: Towards a socially responsible zoonotic disease control. *Zoonoses and Public Health, 66*(1), 26–34.

Whitelaw, S., Mamas, M. A., Topol, E., & Van Spall, H. G. (2020). Applications of digital technology in COVID-19 pandemic planning and response. *The Lancet Digital Health, 2*(8), e435–e440.

Wildlife Conservation Society. (2004). *One world-One Health: Building interdisciplinary bridges.* Retrieved May 22, 2019, from http://www.oneworldonehealth.org/sept2004/owoh_sept04.html

Wilkinson, M. D., Sansone, S. A., Schultes, E., Doorn, P., da Silva, B., Santos, L. O., & Dumontier, M. (2018). A design framework and exemplar metrics for FAIRness. *Scientific Data, 5*(1), 1–4.

Word Health Organization. (1948). Preamble to the Constitution of the World Health Organization as adopted by the International Health Conference, New York, 19–22 June, 1946; signed on 22 July 1946 by the representatives of 61 States.

Xie, T., Liu, W., Anderson, B. D., Liu, X., & Gray, G. C. (2017). A system dynamics approach to understanding the One Health concept. *PLoS One, 12*(9), e0184430.

Zinsstag, J., Schelling, E., Waltner-Toews, D., & Tanner, M. (2011). From "one medicine" to "one health" and systemic approaches to health and well-being. *Preventive Veterinary Medicine, 101*(3–4), 148–156.

Zinsstag, J., Schelling, E., Waltner-Toews, D., Whittaker, M., & Tanner, M. (2015). One Health: The added value of integrated health approaches. CAB International, https://doi.org/10.1079/9781780643410.0000.

CHAPTER 4

Value-Based Healthcare

Abstract The traditional model of care is undergoing radical transformations to face emerging challenges that impact businesses and society. Technological innovation and collaboration are at the center of interest for ensuring resilience, guaranteeing real-time decision-making and business continuity. The crucial aspect of this transformation is the pursuit of Value-Based Healthcare (VBHC) [Porter, M. E. Value-based health care: From idea to reality. In *International Consortium for Health Outcomes Measurement (ICHOM) annual conference* (2013).] and a patient-centricity approach based on value/outcome rather than volume/performance. The strategic Value Agenda aims at moving from a fragmented system to an integrated one that focuses on creating value for patients. This chapter illustrates a theoretical framework for implementing VBHC with the aim to maximize value for patients.

Keywords Value-based healthcare • Value transformation • Patient focus

The traditional model of care is undergoing radical transformations to face emerging challenges (Schiavone & Ferretti, 2021; Durrani, 2016). The pandemic has caused considerable disruptions to the healthcare sector, with marked impacts on businesses and society (Liu et al., 2022). In a time

M. Toni, G. Mattia, *The Digital Healthcare Revolution*, https://doi.org/10.1007/978-3-031-16340-1_4

29

of crisis, technological innovation and collaboration are at the center of interest (Hou & Shi, 2021; Shi et al., 2021). Innovation strategies, shared efforts, and collaborative approaches are essential for ensuring resilience, guaranteeing real-time decision-making and business continuity (Vermicelli et al., 2021; Verma & Gustafsson, 2020; Bem et al., 2019). In this scenario, organizations have to react rapidly to challenges and accommodate new needs considering existing and emerging barriers. Hence, business models should adapt to new market conditions (Am et al., 2020).

The crucial aspect of this transformation is the pursuit of Value-Based Healthcare (VBHC) (Porter, 2013) and patient centricity based on value/ outcome rather than volume/performance. The strategic Value Agenda aims at moving from a fragmented system to an integrated one that focuses on creating value for patients by understanding, analyzing, measuring, and improving the related clinical and functional outcomes. It requires rethinking the model and tracking the patients' pathways to overcome the silos structure. Instead of focusing on processes, efforts should be directed toward creating as much value as possible for the patient in terms of healthcare quality, patients' suffering reduction, improved patient safety, and better cost-effectiveness (Porter & Teisberg, 2006). From a network perspective, all the stakeholders cover a key role, especially clinicians, in implementing VBHC and creating value for the patients.

Porter and Teisberg (2006) introduce the Value Agenda that enlightens potential ways to address the transformation of the healthcare system. From their vision, the overarching goal in healthcare delivery is the achievement of high value for patients. The authors also provide a multifaceted definition of value: from an accountability perspective, value is defined as the health outcomes achieved per money spent, whereas from a managerial perspective, it concerns processes and organization changes. However, the meaning of "Value" can vary because it can differ between stakeholders' perspectives (patients, clinicians, healthcare providers, policymakers, and healthcare companies). This approach focuses on maximizing value for patients, aiming to optimize outcomes and minimize costs. It means building a system around the patient's experience and the related needs, measuring their achievement.

VBHC involves also managerial and technological competencies, and it implies a systemic logic based on value improvement rather than cost containment, outcome rather than volume, organizational integration rather than separated silos, and partnership rather than single selling. Hence, besides cost reduction, the outcomes achieved should be considered for effective care. The European Commission defines the VBHC as a multidimensional concept based on the offering of appropriate care to achieve patients' goals (personal value), on achieving the best possible results with the available resources (technical value), on equally distributing resources to all patient groups (allocative value), on contributing to social participation and connectedness (social value).

Access per se does not constitute value because there could be situations in which patients access ineffective, inadequate, or inefficient care. The fundamental principles that emerge from a VBHC underpinning solidarity approach and a fair distribution of resources are accessibility, equity, quality, performance, and efficiency.

Some important premises have to be noted. The concept of solidarity is the basis of European healthcare systems by securing universal access to affordable, preventive, curative, and high-quality healthcare in the EU (Charter of Fundamental Rights of the European Union and the European Pillar of Social Rights). Hence, the primary goal should be the value, and improving value is essential to make access affordable.

Porter (2013) proposes a strategic agenda with six distinct but mutually reinforcing components of the value agenda for moving to a high-value healthcare delivery system:

1. Organization of integrated assistance units (Integrated Practice Units— IPUs): changing the way clinicians are organized to deliver care (from silos organization to a structure built around the patient's medical condition). An IPU, a dedicated multidisciplinary team composed of clinical and non-clinical personnel, provides the entire care cycle for the patient's condition.
2. Measurement of outcomes and costs for each patient: outcomes should be measured by medical condition rather than specialty or intervention. Moreover, outcomes should cover the entire care cycle, tracking the patient's health status after care is completed.
3. The implementation of reimbursements for care processes: Porter and Lee (2013) state that the payment approach consistent with measuring value is a bundled payment in which the payment is linked to the overall patient care. Bundled payments have several benefits by encouraging teamwork, increasing high-value care, and improving efficiency and outcome.
4. Integration of care assistance across separate facilities: integrating systems eliminates the fragmentation and duplication of care and opti-

mizes the types of care delivered in each location; indeed, there is a growing number of multisite healthcare delivery organizations; thus, integrating care for individual patients across locations and sites provides opportunities for improving value. IPUs should manage care and the entire care cycle among different sites by adopting integrating mechanisms.

5. Exceeding the geographical limit: geographic expansion should focus on improving value instead of volume. There are two types of geographic expansion: the hub-and-spoke model and the clinical affiliation. In the hub-and-spoke model, satellite facilities are established for each IPU and clinicians rotate among locations (improving team working). In the clinical affiliation, an IPU uses the facilities of community providers or other local organizations, providing management oversight for clinical care.

6. Building and enabling an effective IT platform: a supporting information technology platform allows the achievement of the previous points. Since healthcare IT systems have been applied on a silos model, it needs to be reconsidered in order to follow patients in their entire cycle of care (patients' journey) across services, sites/departments, including hospitalization, outpatient visits, physical therapy, and other interventions. Hence, data need to be aggregated around patients. The main requirements are building an IT platform centered on patients that manages all types of patient data using a common data definition, with medical records accessible to all parties involved in the care and equipped with expert systems for each medical condition.

Based on Porter's vision, these six components of the value agenda allow moving toward a high-value healthcare delivery system. These components can interact with each other without necessarily following a specific order. Progress will be most significant if multiple components are advanced together.

Other authors, such as Teisberg et al. (2020), define a framework to guide organizations in building VBHC systems. This transformation requires several steps that are described as follows:

- Understand shared health needs of patients: healthcare should be organized around segments of patients with a shared set of health (clinical and non-clinical) needs and with a particular medical condition. In this way, care shifts from treating to solving patients' needs. It allows to meet and efficiently anticipate patient needs.

- Design a comprehensive solution for health outcomes improvement: on the basis of the previous step, teams design and deliver care consistently to optimize care by providing health services in an integrated way, overcoming fragmentation and duplication of care. Patient care needs to be integrated, managing the entire care cycle and removing obstacles that undermine patients' health.
- Integrate learning teams: this new approach changes how clinicians are organized to deliver care, promoting an integrated multidisciplinary team that manages the entire pathway.
- Measure health outcomes and costs: outcomes should track the patient status/progress and cover the entire care cycle. It is possible to divide the outcomes into clinical outcomes (evaluating whether the therapies are consistent with the expectations) and functional outcomes related to the quality of life (informing about the patient functional ability after the treatment).
- Expand partnerships: partnerships can create opportunities for shared goals of creating high value by integrating patient care needs across locations and sites.

Van der Nat (2021) observes some best practices, noticing that healthcare providers that adopt the principles of VBHC are implementing one or some of these dimensions. Thus, the opportunity to accomplish the transformation from volume to value is reinforced if multiple dimensions are implemented simultaneously. However, implementing a technological solution is crucial since it supports and enables a system based on VBHC. Porter and Teisberg (2006) state that building and enabling an effective information technology platform is necessary for pursuing VBHC. An integrated IT system allows the achievement of the previous five dimensions by tracking the entire care cycle, sharing information and communication across facilities and locations. Innovating through an IT platform needs to be centered on patients, to manage and record different types of data, and to be easily accessible and comprehensible to all the stakeholders involved. The infrastructure has to be rearranged in order to follow the patient journey (patient pathway) across services, departments, and facilities.

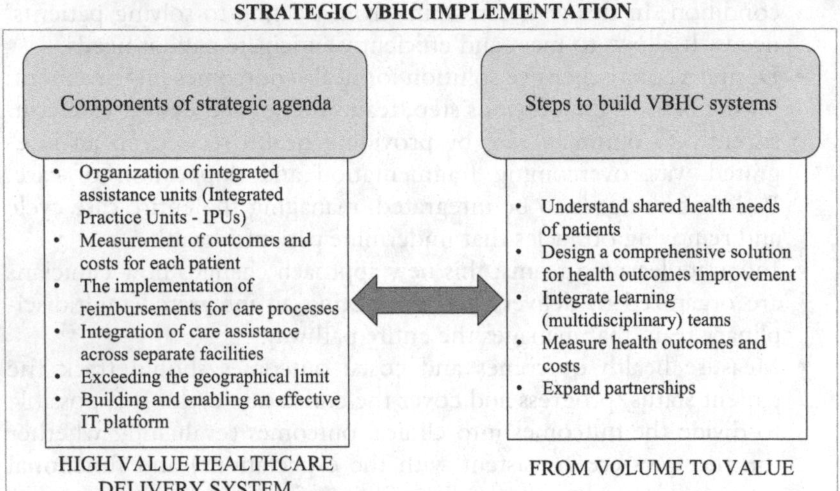

STRATEGIC VBHC IMPLEMENTATION

Components of strategic agenda

- Organization of integrated assistance units (Integrated Practice Units - IPUs)
- Measurement of outcomes and costs for each patient
- The implementation of reimbursements for care processes
- Integration of care assistance across separate facilities
- Exceeding the geographical limit
- Building and enabling an effective IT platform

HIGH VALUE HEALTHCARE
DELIVERY SYSTEM

Steps to build VBHC systems

- Understand shared health needs of patients
- Design a comprehensive solution for health outcomes improvement
- Integrate learning (multidisciplinary) teams
- Measure health outcomes and costs
- Expand partnerships

FROM VOLUME TO VALUE

Fig. 4.1 Strategic implementation of value-based healthcare

Fig. 4.1 illustrates the strategic implementation of VBHC, by merging the contribution of Teisberg et al. (2020) with the one of Porter and Teisberg (2006).

Based on Andersson et al.'s (2015) contribution, we propose a general framework for VBHC. A VBHC approach allows to focus on what creates value for patients, improving their experience of care; this approach allows also to organize the care around patients' medical conditions and entire pathway, following and tracking the patient's journey. At last, following this approach, medical outcomes need to be measured to improve population's health and cost efficiency. Implementing all the components of VBHC means working on improving patients' outcomes and optimizing patients' pathways to deliver high-value care.

Figure 4.2 shows the general framework of VBHC.

The transformation toward a value-based organization involves all the stakeholders: clinicians, services providers, patients, employees, and suppliers that can all jointly enable and benefit from the potential scenario. On this purpose, it is necessary to highlight the importance of creating awareness about leadership and change management topics with training

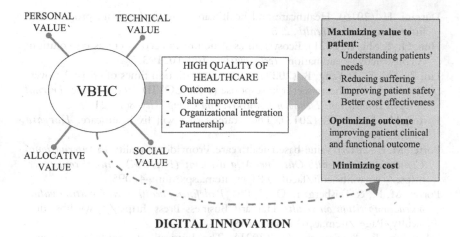

PERSONAL VALUE

TECHNICAL VALUE

VBHC

HIGH QUALITY OF HEALTHCARE
- Outcome
- Value improvement
- Organizational integration
- Partnership

ALLOCATIVE VALUE

SOCIAL VALUE

Maximizing value to patient:
- Understanding patients' needs
- Reducing suffering
- Improving patient safety
- Better cost effectiveness

Optimizing outcome
improving patient clinical and functional outcome

Minimizing cost

DIGITAL INNOVATION

Fig. 4.2 General framework of VBHC

and education for developing new competencies. This action will be essential to build a common framework in which all the stakeholders of the network will be aligned toward the patient centricity vision.

The next chapter (Chap. 5) examines the value cocreation concept applied to healthcare, implying the stakeholders' engagement toward the common goal of patient centricity.

REFERENCES

Am, J. B., Furstenthal, L., Jorge, F., & Roth, E. (2020). *Innovation in a crisis: Why it is more critical than ever*. Retrieved June, 17, 2021. https://www.mckinsey.com/~/media/McKinsey/Business%20Functions/Strategy%20and%20Corporate%20Finance/Our%20Insights/Innovation%20in%20a%20crisis%20Why%20it%20is%20more%20critical%20than%20ever/Innovation-in-a-crisis-Why-it-is-more-critical-than-ever-vF.pdf

Andersson, A. E., Bååthe, F., Wikström, E., & Nilsson, K. (2015). Understanding value-based healthcare–an interview study with project team members at a Swedish university hospital. *Journal of Hospital Administration, 4*(4), 64–72.

Bem, A., Siedlecki, R., Prędkiewicz, P., Gazzola, P., Ryszawska, B., & Ucieklak-Jeż, P. (2019). Hospitals' financial health in rural and urban areas in Poland: Does it ensure sustainability? *Sustainability, 11*(7), 1932.

Durrani, H. (2016). Healthcare and healthcare systems: Inspiring progress and future prospects. *Mhealth, 2*, 3.

Hou, H., & Shi, Y. (2021). Ecosystem-as-structure and ecosystem-as-coevolution: A constructive examination. *Technovation, 100*, 102193.

Liu, Z., Shi, Y., & Yang, B. (2022). Open innovation in times of crisis: An overview of the healthcare sector in response to the COVID-19 pandemic. *Journal of Open Innovation: Technology, Market, and Complexity, 8*(1), 21.

Porter, M., & Lee, T. (2013). The strategy that will fix healthcare. *Harvard Business Review*.

Porter, M. E. (2013). Value-based health care: From idea to reality. In *International Consortium for Health Outcomes Measurement (ICHOM) annual conference*. https://www.hbs.edu/faculty/Pages/item.aspx?num=47095

Porter, M. E., & Teisberg, E. O. (2006). *Redefining health care: Creating value-based competition on results*. Harvard Business Press. https://www.hbs.edu/faculty/Pages/item.aspx?num=21319

Schiavone, F., & Ferretti, M. (2021). The FutureS of healthcare. *Futures, 134*, 102849.

Shi, Y., Lu, C., Hou, H., Zhen, L., & Hu, J. (2021). Linking business ecosystem and natural ecosystem together—A sustainable pathway for future industrialization. *Journal of Open Innovation: Technology, Market, and Complexity, 7*(1), 38.

Teisberg, E., Wallace, S., & O'Hara, S. (2020). Defining and implementing value-based health care: A strategic framework. *Academic Medicine, 95*(5), 682.

van der Nat, P. B. (2021). The new strategic agenda for value transformation. *Health Services Management Research, 35*, 189. https://doi.org/10.1177/09514848211011739

Verma, S., & Gustafsson, A. (2020). Investigating the emerging COVID-19 research trends in the field of business and management: A bibliometric analysis approach. *Journal of Business Research, 118*, 253–261.

Vermicelli, S., Cricelli, L., & Grimaldi, M. (2021). How can crowdsourcing help tackle the COVID-19 pandemic? An explorative overview of innovative collaborative practices. *R&D Management, 51*(2), 183–194.

CHAPTER 5

Value Co-creation and Stakeholders' Engagement

Abstract Healthcare innovation should include an improvement of customer value co-creation toward a more experiential and systemic understanding of value creation. In this view, multiple actors integrate resources to offer value to the entire population in terms of health services. Healthcare value co-creation supposes that patients act as resource integrators and active co-creators of value, in collaboration with healthcare professionals. The focus of innovation should move from products and services to experiences involving different actors in exchanging resources to satisfy patients' needs and outcomes. Following the value co-creation approach, the healthcare context needs to rethink the offering with the lens of patient experience and patient centricity.

Digitization is a lever for empowering patients by facilitating the exchange with healthcare professionals and minimizing barriers.

This chapter provides theoretical insights into value co-creation in healthcare.

Keywords Value co-creation • Innovation • Stakeholders' engagement • Patients' involvement • Collaboration

New business models in healthcare have to face the multifaceted concept of innovation, in which proposing only a new offering is not enough; indeed, innovation should include an improvement of customer value co-creation (Rubalcaba et al., 2012), beyond traditional output and process-based archetypes to a more experiential/systemic understanding of value creation (Karpen et al., 2012; Prahalad & Ramaswamy, 2003). The healthcare systems are increasingly patient-centered and adopt collaborative care models (Sweeney et al., 2015). The systemic archetype is particularly suitable for the healthcare system because it embeds a holistic approach in which multiple actors integrate resources to offer value to the entire population in terms of health services. Opportunities for organizations in this environment arise with the aim of connecting with multiple stakeholders to sustain the network (Helkkula et al., 2018). In the healthcare context, the definition of a service ecosystem can be particularly applicable to the healthcare context because it is a self-contained and self-adjusting system of resource-integrating actors connected by shared institutional logics and mutual value creation through service exchange (Lusch & Vargo, 2014). A service ecosystem has a twofold role: enabling value co-creation and fostering service innovation (Edvardsson & Tronvoll, 2013). By merging these two concepts, instead of focusing on processes, healthcare innovation should be directed toward creating the best value for the patient in relation to cost (Porter & Teisberg, 2006; Lee & Porter, 2013). Pursuing this transformation is an overarching strategy that will require restructuring how healthcare delivery is organized and measured.

In line with Service-Dominant (SD) logic, Rubalcaba et al. (2012) suggested that the logic of co-creation should focus primarily on the co-creation of value rather than on the service offering or output. In SD logic, value co-creation is, thus, considered an outcome of resource integration; in fact, co-created value occurs in any case in which two or more actors integrate their resources (Kleinaltenkamp et al., 2012). Healthcare service co-production and value co-creation suppose that the patient is treated as an active co-creator of value (Krisjanous & Maude, 2014; McColl-Kennedy et al., 2017; Nambisan & Nambisan, 2009; Osei-Frimpong et al., 2015), consistently with the patient-centric lens. The patient is recognized as a prosumer of healthcare, actively acting as a resource integrator and value co-creator in collaboration with healthcare professionals (Osei-Frimpong & Owusu-Frimpong, 2017). By applying the assumption of Prahalad and Ramaswamy (2003), the focus of innovation should move from products and services to experience involving the entire healthcare network (hospitals, clinics, organizations, proximity structures) and individuals (clinicians, healthcare professionals, caregivers, patients) to co-create unique value to the community. It implies the engagement of different actors in exchanging resources to satisfy patients' needs and outcomes. On this view, value resides in the experience of co-creation in service ecosystems, supported by service processes and implemented as outputs. The active participation of patients is acknowledged to lead to benefits in terms of medical outcomes, lower costs, more effective and efficient service delivery, increased quality and satisfaction (Gallan et al., 2013), and the personalization of healthcare services (Lattemann, 2020; Vogus & McClelland, 2016).

Helkkula et al. (2018) present a four-stage process to pursue a value-centric approach to service innovation that can be applied to the healthcare context. At first, the four archetypes should be identified by analyzing their potential for improving value co-creation with patients and other relevant stakeholders. Once identified opportunities for innovation, the optimal combination of archetypes and approaches to value creation has to be examined (value-in-exchange, value-in-use, value-in-experience, value-in-context). Resources and capabilities need to be deployed to facilitate value co-creation with patients and stakeholders. Evaluation of the different archetype combinations should be conducted before, during, and after service innovation implementation. Each archetype can contribute individually to value, but their integration allows to achieve a value-centric view.

The value-centric approach can be applied to any actor's perspective; however, healthcare service innovation focuses on patient-centric vision (see Chap. 6). It is important to understand how individual patients perceive the value co-created in a given service ecosystem made of resources and actors integration (value-in-context), how new services can be developed by applying new ideas or current thinking in different ways (value-in-use), how novel output is created with valuable attributes of service innovation (value-in-exchange), or how living valuable experiences that are individually experienced but socially co-created (value-in-experience) (Helkkula et al., 2018).

Figure 5.1 integrates innovation and value co-creation concepts.

Resource integration is required for value co-creation (Virléè et al., 2020). Service users are considered resource integrators because they interact in activities that facilitate or create value (Hibbert et al., 2012).

In order to achieve a value-centric approach, firms have to design resources integration mechanisms to link resources, actors, and institutional arrangements aimed at value co-creation and service innovation. By applying this argument to healthcare, patients change from being recipients of treatments to becoming active actors, co-producers of health

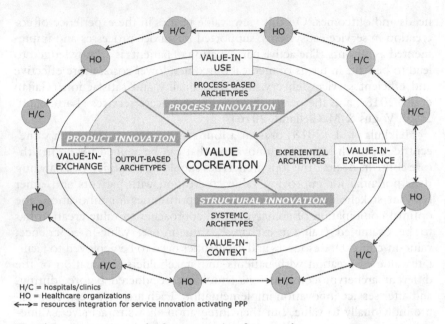

Fig. 5.1 Innovation and value co-creation framework

services, and co-creators of value (Palumbo, 2017). This active participation results in a co-creation process in which patients and professionals cooperate to solve problems (Osei-Frimpong et al., 2018; Tartaglione et al., 2018; Dalal et al., 2016).

Following the value co-creation approach, the healthcare context needs to rethink the offering with the lens of patient experience and the pursuit of patient centricity. The patients' involvement in the process (i.e., in integrating the resources) is crucial because they substantially affect the related outcomes (Busse et al., 2010). Patients' resource integration activities can thus be considered key determinants of healthcare outcomes (McColl-Kennedy et al., 2017).

In the case of chronic diseases, co-creation process becomes even more relevant. In fact, chronic diseases require treatment with the active participation of patients and their families in order to find the best tailor-made solutions (Sagner et al., 2017; Auffray et al., 2010). Moreover, the integration of the patient's own resources with resources from friends, family, other patients, and multiple service providers is also necessary for value co-creation (Beirão et al., 2017; Danaher & Gallan, 2016) along with the involvement of clinicians to ensure monitoring and continuity of care.

Patient participation is always recognized with patients being instructed without being overburdened with information (European Medicines Agency, 2013); however, the centric view of patients' engagement is moving toward empowerment and autonomy in managing their health. However, it has to be considered that service users have different abilities to perform the required integration activities (Hibbert et al., 2012), thus cocreating value implies also making accessible relevant information for managing health and creating an open communication channel between healthcare professionals and patients.

Value co-creation should be investigated from a management perspective to facilitate comprehension of the multifaceted value creation and which actor contributes the most. This process has to be examined from the individual perspective of the actors that directly interact with healthcare services and are aware of gaps and potential needs for improvements. On this strength, individuals who interact the most in the healthcare context are clinicians, employees, patients, and caregivers/families. Patients' engagement in value co-creation model and their interactions with all the actors of the network (clinicians, nurses, healthcare professionals, caregivers, families) should be considered (Zhang et al., 2015). With globalization and technological advancements, customers and service providers become more connected. The key for successful value co-creation depends on the quality of interactions between service providers and customers (Aarikka-Stenroos & Jaakkola, 2012).

As Chap. 4 explains, in the healthcare service system, reduced costs and time associated with treatments can no longer fully illustrate the value of health service (Porter, 2010). All actors' engagement becomes crucial in light of the switch from passive patients to active co-creators in health service (Nordgren, 2009; Witell et al., 2011). Digitization is the key to patients' involvement in co-generating health data and fostering participation in healthcare decision-making (Aquino et al., 2018; Ciasullo et al., 2022). Digitization empowers patients by facilitating the exchange with healthcare professionals and minimizing cognitive burdens, physical and time constraints. An example can be represented by e-health tools which ensure access to comprehensive support and patients' assistance; in this way, by providing both functional assistance and social/emotional support, patients' activation as prosumers in value co-creation is ensured by increasing patients' awareness, health protection, and risk prevention

(Roeper et al., 2018). Furthermore, digital tools can strengthen the therapeutic adherence to medical indications through notifications—such as text messaging, recommendations, and updates—addressed to patients (Biederman et al., 2019).

In literature, the design of a digital-based healthcare delivery system for value co-creation is established on four layers: cognitive, social, technological, and emotional determinants of patient empowerment (Ciasullo et al., 2022; Fico et al., 2015) as it is possible to observe in the Fig. 5.2.

Developing digital solutions directed at patient empowerment and involvement enables a boundaryless approach to healthcare. However, digitization causes a lack of human touch that can inhibit trust and decrease the willingness toward engagement (Blandford, 2019). Hence, planning a digital interaction with health services in a patient-centric perspective requires a co-creation approach that includes both patients and healthcare professionals (de Souza et al., 2017). It implies the alignment of offering and demand perspectives in relation to service provision, encouraging customization based on specific needs. This approach requires organizational arrangement by enabling initiatives to continuously engage

DIGITAL-BASED HEALTHCARE DELIVERY SYSTEM FOR VALUE COCREATION

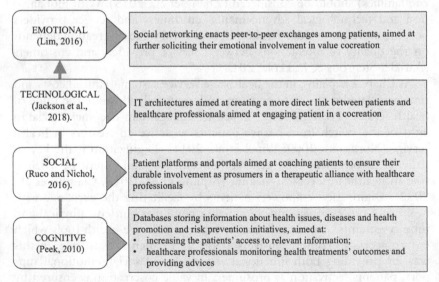

Fig. 5.2 Layers of digital system for implementing value co-creation

patients as prosumers, to train and actively involve healthcare professionals toward a service co-creation approach (Batalden et al., 2016).

Besides digital resources, implementing value co-creation requires a networked approach in which healthcare providers encourage patients' participation (Brambini & Vang, 2018). Boosting the patient's ability to seek adequate health-related information, process available information to make timely decisions, and navigate the healthcare system, digital communities foster the shift from patient education to patient engagement and, thus, from consumers to prosumers of healthcare (Gruman et al., 2010). Moreover, they solicit the patients' understanding of health issues and stimulate awareness and behavioral changes (Guarneri et al., 2016), positively contributing to health outcomes (McDonald et al., 2013).

In previous healthcare research, innovative strategies for patient engagement have been based on patients' feedback tools such as diaries and questionnaires for collecting information about service improvements (Zhang et al., 2015; Elg et al., 2012). This type of data collection often is administered during the entire patient journey until the treatment is finished (including waiting for treatment, diagnosis, treatment, and after treatment). The advantage of this approach is that the value co-created will be delivered to the patient through an improved treatment based on data analysis. The basic idea is to improve the lower-rating service and to compare the high-rating services to develop standard services on which healthcare providers and clinicians need to be trained. Patients' feedback should be collected and analyzed in a systematic way to co-create value (Zhang et al., 2015). By gaining feedback from patients, a direct communication channel is built between patients and clinicians to understand service quality and co-create service value. The outcomes of patient empowerment should be continuously monitored to propose timely initiatives to sustain the patients' participation (Singh et al., 2018; Ciasullo et al., 2022).

The importance of engaging health professionals in sustaining processes of organizational learning, change, and innovation has been emphasized by scholars and practitioners (Øygarden et al., 2020; Lega & Palumbo, 2021). Indeed, employees' engagement in healthcare organizations enhances organizational performances (Lowe, 2012) and sustains productivity in complex situations and turbulent environmental conditions (Palumbo, 2021). The positive impact of employees' engagement on the improvement of organizational performance primarily progresses through the individual and collective readiness to embrace innovation and change (Arshi & Rao, 2019). It is worth noting that employees' engagement and participation in innovation are mutually related in a virtuous cycle, with engagement triggering a greater propensity to innovate and participation in innovation nurturing the engagement at work of employees (Hollebeek et al., 2018).

At the individual level, a systemic feedback tool model should consider the perspectives of all actors directly interacting. Hence, different feedback tools need to be customized on the basis of the target respondents (clinicians, nurses, healthcare professionals, patients, caregivers, and families) and then build a comprehensive model that includes multiple perspectives for identifying opportunities of improvements.

In Fig. 5.3, it is possible to observe the individual actors that are engaged in the healthcare value co-creation process; moreover, hospitals, clinics, and healthcare organizations revolve around this value co-creation process, by proposing innovative solutions, quality improvement solutions, and reorganization in line with actors' needs (Sabadosa & Batalden, 2014).

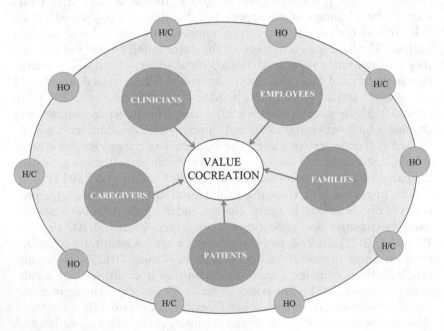

Fig. 5.3 Actors engaging in value co-creation

Four value co-creation models have been defined in healthcare: Partnership, Diffusion, Open Source, and Support Group (Nambisan & Nambisan, 2009).

The Partnership aims at improving existing care delivery models or creating new models through the active and informed participation of parents and families on the care team as participants in care programs. The Diffusion model informs knowledge about new delivery models throughout the network and communication. The Open Source model entails creating new knowledge through accessing and sharing outcome data or important information with both patients and other care facilities. The Support group implies the sharing of experiential knowledge with families of patients participating in the development and conduct of education and support.

This change of view toward patient centricity and value co-creation models could also be enabled by the readiness of patients to take more responsibility for their health and to collaborate with healthcare professionals (Lattemann, 2020; Aggarwal & Basu, 2014; Elg et al., 2012; Sweeney et al., 2015). Nonetheless, to enable this transformation and become co-creators, patients ought to be supported by suitable processes, methods, and tools that enable their active role in healthcare design and delivery (Elg et al., 2012; Stiggelbout et al., 2012). This requires new knowledge and skills and new dispositions of healthcare professionals (Batalden et al., 2015) as well as a change in attitudes and behavior, often based on the traditional view of professional superiority (Lattemann, 2020; Cayton, 2006).

A participatory approach to organizational change is required to implement transition and should be based on a dialog involving all those affected by the process of transformation (Palumbo, 2021; Myall et al., 2020).

REFERENCES

Aarikka-Stenroos, L., & Jaakkola, E. (2012). Value co-creation in knowledge intensive business services: A dyadic perspective on the joint problem solving process. *Industrial Marketing Management, 41*(1), 15–26.

Aggarwal, P., & Basu, A. K. (2014). Value co-creation: Factors affecting discretionary effort exertion. *Services Marketing Quarterly, 35*(4), 321–336.

Aquino, R. P., Barile, S., Grasso, A., & Saviano, M. (2018). Envisioning smart and sustainable healthcare: 3D Printing technologies for personalized medication. *Futures, 103*, 35–50.

Arshi, T., & Rao, V. (2019). Assessing impact of employee engagement on innovation and the mediating role of readiness for innovation. *International Journal of Comparative Management, 2*(2), 174–202.

Auffray, C., Charron, D., & Hood, L. (2010). Predictive, preventive, personalized and participatory medicine: Back to the future. *Genome Medicine, 2*(8), 1–3.

Batalden, M., Batalden, P., Margolis, P., et al. (2015). Coproduction of healthcare service. *BMJ Quality & Safety.* https://doi.org/10.1136/bmjqs-2015-004315

Batalden, M., Batalden, P., Margolis, P., Seid, M., Armstrong, G., Opipari-Arrigan, L., & Hartung, H. (2016). Coproduction of healthcare service. BMJ quality & safety, 25(7), 509–517.

Beirão, G., Patrício, L., & Fisk, R. P. (2017). Value cocreation in service ecosystems: Investigating health care at the micro, meso, and macro levels. *Journal of Service Management, 28*, 227–249.

Biederman, J., Fried, R., DiSalvo, M., Woodworth, K. Y., Biederman, I., Noyes, E., Faraone, S. V., & Perlis, R. H. (2019). A novel text message intervention to improve adherence to stimulants in adults with attention deficit/hyperactivity disorder. *Journal of Clinical Psychopharmacology, 39*(1), 351–356.

Blandford, A. (2019). HCI for health and wellbeing: Challenges and opportunities. *International Journal of Human-Computer Studies, 131*(1), 41–51.

Brambini, A., & Vang, J. (2018). Towards a networked governance approach in Danish hospitals? Analysing the role of patients in solving wicked problems. *World Review of Entrepreneurship, Management and Sustainable Development, 14*(3), 291–311.

Busse, R., Scheller-Kreinsen, D., & Zentner, A. (2010). *Tackling chronic disease in Europe: Strategies, interventions and challenges (no. 20).* WHO Regional Office Europe.

Cayton, H. (2006). The flat-pack patient? Creating health together. *Patient Education and Counseling, 62*(3), 288–290.

Ciasullo, M. V., Orciuoli, F., Douglas, A., & Palumbo, R. (2022). Putting Health 4.0 at the service of Society 5.0: Exploratory insights from a pilot study. *Socio-Economic Planning Sciences, 80*, 101163.

Dalal, A. K., Dykes, P. C., Collins, S., Lehmann, L. S., Ohashi, K., Rozenblum, R., et al. (2016). A web-based, patient-centered toolkit to engage patients and caregivers in the acute care setting: A preliminary evaluation. *Journal of the American Medical Informatics Association, 23*(1), 80–87.

Danaher, T. S., & Gallan, A. S. (2016). Service research in health care: Positively impacting lives. *Journal of Service Research, 19*(4), 433–437.

de Souza, S., Galloway, J., Simpson, C., Chura, R., Dobson, J., Gullick, N. J., Steer, S., & Lempp, H. (2017). Patient involvement in rheumatology outpatient service design and delivery: A case study. *Health Expectations, 20*(3), 508–518.

Edvardsson, B., & Tronvoll, B. (2013). A new conceptualization of service innovation grounded in S-D logic and service systems. *International Journal of Quality and Service Sciences, 5,* 19–31.

Elg, M., Engström, J., Witell, L., & Poksinka, B. (2012). Co-creation and learning in health-care service development. *Journal of Service Management, 23*(3), 328–343.

European Medicines Agency. (2013, October 18). The patient's voice in the evaluation of medicines. How patients can contribute to the assessment of benefit and risk. Retrieved January 2017, from http://www.ema.europa.eu/docs/en_GB/document_library/Report/2013/10/WC500153276.pdf

Fico, G., Gaeta, E., Arredondo, M.T. and Pecchia, L. (2015), "Analytic hierarchy process to define the most important factors and related technologies for empowering elderly people in taking an active role in their health", *Journal of Medical Systems, 39*(9), Article 98.

Gallan, A. S., Jarvis, C. B., Brown, S. W., & Bitner, M. J. (2013). Customer positivity and participation in services: An empirical test in a health care context. *Journal of the Academy of Marketing Science, 41*(3), 338–356.

Gruman, J., Rovner, M. H., French, M. E., Jeffress, D., Sofaer, S., Shaller, D., & Prager, D. J. (2010). From patient education to patient engagement: Implications for the field of patient education. *Patient Education and Counseling, 78*(3), 350–356.

Guarneri, M. R., Brocca, M. D., & Piras, L. (2016). Patient's empowerment and behaviour change: Complementary approaches in EU projects PALANTE and PEGASO. In *EAI international conference on Personal, Pervasive and Mobile Health, Budapest.*

Helkkula, A., Kowalkowski, C., & Tronvoll, B. (2018). Archetypes of service innovation: Implications for value cocreation. *Journal of Service Research, 21*(3), 284–301.

Hibbert, S., Winklhofer, H., & Temerak, M. S. (2012). Customers as resource integrators: Toward a model of customer learning. *Journal of Service Research, 15*(3), 247–261.

Hollebeek, L. D., Andreassen, T. W., Smith, D. L., Grönquist, D., Karahasanovic, A., & Marquez, A. (2018). Epilogue–service innovation actor engagement: An integrative model. *Journal of Services Marketing, 32*(1), 95–100.

Karpen, I. O., Bove, L. L., & Lukas, B. A. (2012). Linking service-dominant logic and strategic business practice: A conceptual model of a service-dominant orientation. *Journal of Service Research, 15*(1), 21–38.

Kleinaltenkamp, M., Brodie, R. J., Frow, P., Hughes, T., Peters, L. D., & Woratschek, H. (2012). *Resource integration. Marketing Theory, 12*(2), 201–205.

Krisjanous, J., & Maude, R. (2014). Customer value co-creation within partnership models of health care: An examination of the New Zealand Midwifery Partnership Model. *Australasian Marketing Journal (AMJ), 22*(3), 230–237.

Lattemann, C. (2020). Rezension "Human-centered digitalization and services". In *HMD Praxis der Wirtschaftsinformatik* (Vol. 57, p. 4). Springer.

Lee, T., & Porter, M. (2013). The strategy that will fix healthcare. *Harvard Business Review.*

Lega, F., & Palumbo, R. (2021). Leading through the 'new normality' of health care. *Health Services Management Research, 34*(1), 47–52.

Lowe, G. (2012). How employee engagement matters for hospital performance. *Healthcare Quarterly, 15*(2), 29–39.

Lusch, R. F., & Vargo, S. L. (2014). *The service-dominant logic of marketing: Dialog, debate, and directions.* Routledge.

McColl-Kennedy, J. R., Hogan, S. J., Witell, L., & Snyder, H. (2017). Cocreative customer practices: Effects of health care customer value cocreation practices on well-being. *Journal of Business Research, 70,* 55–66.

McDonald, E. M., Frattaroli, S., Kromm, E. E., Ma, X., Pike, M., & Holtgrave, D. (2013). Improvements in health behaviors and health status among newly insured members of an innovative health access plan. *Journal of Community Health, 38*(2), 301–309.

Myall, M., May, C., Richardson, A., Bogle, S., Campling, N., Dace, S. and Lund, S. (2020), "Creating preconditions for change in clinical practice: the influence of interactions between multiple contexts and human agency", Journal of Health Organization and Management, Vol. 35 No. 9, pp. 1–17.

Nambisan, P., & Nambisan, S. (2009). Models of consumer value cocreation in health care. *Health Care Management Review, 34*(4), 344–354.

Nordgren, L. (2009). Value creation in health care services–developing service productivity: Experiences from Sweden. *International Journal of Public Sector Management, 22,* 114.

Osei-Frimpong, K., & Owusu-Frimpong, N. (2017). Value co-creation in health care: A phenomenological examination of the doctor-patient encounter. *Journal of Nonprofit & Public Sector Marketing, 29*(4), 365–384.

Osei-Frimpong, K., Wilson, A., & Lemke, F. (2018). Patient co-creation activities in healthcare service delivery at the micro level: The influence of online access to healthcare information. *Technological Forecasting and Social Change, 126,* 14–27.

Osei-Frimpong, K., Wilson, A., & Owusu-Frimpong, N. (2015). Service experiences and dyadic value co-creation in healthcare service delivery: A CIT approach. *Journal of Service Theory and Practice, 25,* 443.

Øygarden, O., Olsen, E., & Mikkelsen, A. (2020). Changing to improve? Organizational change and change-oriented leadership in hospitals. *Journal of Health Organization and Management, 24*(6), 687–706.

Palumbo, R. (2017). Toward a new conceptualization of health care services to inspire public health. Public national health service as a "common pool of resources". *International Review on Public and Nonprofit Marketing,* *14*(3), 271–287.

Palumbo, R. (2021). Leveraging organizational health literacy to enhance health promotion and risk prevention: A narrative and interpretive literature review. *Yale Journal of Biology and Medicine, 94*(1), 115–128.

Porter, M. E. (2010). What is value in health care. *The New England Journal of Medicine, 363*(26), 2477–2481.

Porter, M. E., & Teisberg, E. O. (2006). *Redefining health care: Creating value-based competition on results.* Harvard Business Press.

Prahalad, C. K., & Ramaswamy, V. (2003). The new frontier of experience innovation. *MIT Sloan Management Review, 44*(4), 12.

Roeper, B., Mocko, J., O'Connor, L. M., Zhou, J., Castillo, D., & Beck, E. H. (2018). Mobile integrated healthcare intervention and impact analysis with a Medicare advantage population. *Population Health Management, 21*(5), 349–356.

Rubalcaba, L., Michel, S., Sundbo, J., Brown, S. W., & Reynoso, J. (2012). Shaping, organizing, and rethinking service innovation: A multidimensional framework. *Journal of Service Management, 23*(5), 696–715.

Sabadosa, K. A., & Batalden, P. B. (2014). The interdependent roles of patients, families and professionals in cystic fibrosis: A system for the coproduction of healthcare and its improvement. *BMJ Quality & Safety, 23*(Suppl 1), i90–i94.

Sagner, M., McNeil, A., Puska, P., Auffray, C., Price, N. D., Hood, L., et al. (2017). The P4 health spectrum–a predictive, preventive, personalized and participatory continuum for promoting healthspan. *Progress in Cardiovascular Diseases, 59*(5), 506–521.

Singh, J. B., Chandwani, R., & Kumar, M. (2018). Factors affecting Web 2.0 adoption: Exploring the knowledge sharing and knowledge seeking aspects in health care professionals. *Journal of Knowledge Management, 22*, 21.

Stiggelbout, A. M., Van der Weijden, T., De Wit, M. P., Frosch, D., Légaré, F., Montori, V. M., et al. (2012). Shared decision making: Really putting patients at the centre of healthcare. *BMJ, 344*, e256.

Sweeney, J. S., Danaher, T. S., & McColl-Kennedy, J. R. (2015). Customer effort in value cocreation activities: Improving quality of life and behavioral intentions of healthcare customers. *Journal of Service Research, 53*(9), 1689–1699.

Tartaglione, A. M., Cavacece, Y., Cassia, F., & Russo, G. (2018). The excellence of patient-centered healthcare. *The TQM Journal, 30*, 153.

Virlée, J. B., Hammedi, W., & van Riel, A. C. (2020). Healthcare service users as resource integrators: investigating factors influencing the co-creation of value at individual, dyadic and systemic levels. *Journal of service theory and practice, 30*(3), 277–306.

Vogus, T. J., & McClelland, L. E. (2016). When the customer is the patient: Lessons from healthcare research on patient satisfaction and service quality ratings. *Human Resource Management Review, 26*(1), 37–49.

Witell, L., Kristensson, P., Gustafsson, A., & Löfgren, M. (2011). Idea generation: Customer co-creation versus traditional market research techniques. *Journal of Service Management, 22,* 140.

Zhang, L., Tong, H., Demirel, H. O., Duffy, V. G., Yih, Y., & Bidassie, B. (2015). A practical model of value co-creation in healthcare service. *Procedia Manufacturing, 3,* 200–207.

CHAPTER 6

The Evolution to Patient Centricity

Abstract The aim of this chapter is to provide a comprehensive theoretical framework of patient centricity, encompassing the main definitions. Rethinking the healthcare system with a patient-centric view implies the pursuit of a process composed of the phases of patient activation, empowerment, involvement, and engagement.

The implementation of patient centricity requires a consistent and coordinated approach, in order to make the patients active participants in the decision-making process by identifying their needs and making information accessible. Managerial implications are proposed in the concluding part of the chapter.

Keywords Patient centricity • Digitization • Patients' needs • Patients' engagement

Putting the patients at the center means answering patients' needs and improving their lives in a meaningful way. In the past, healthcare adopted mainly a system-centric model giving particular attention to system efficiencies and metrics (Phillips & Elliott, 2018).

Nowadays, the health system requires to switch its perspective to include network coordination composed of an increasing number of healthcare stakeholders embedding the perspective of patients (Castro et al., 2016). Patients became key actors instead of mere recipients of service (Adinolfi et al., 2016) with the urgent need to acquire more knowledge and an active role in managing their own health. For instance, in the pharmaceutical industry—which is devoted to medicines for the prevention or treatment of disease—involving patients in its processes means a change of perspective from disease-centered to a strategy focused on patients (du Plessis et al., 2017).

As Chap. 5 explains, value co-creation can enable this transition with a participatory approach in healthcare provision. This view overcomes the narrow perspective of centeredness, a static fixed concept in which clinicians invite patients in decision-making only to determine treatments or care (Robbins et al., 2013). The centricity is a broader view that requires a deep understanding of patients' medical conditions, experiences, needs, priorities, and desired outcomes (Hoos et al., 2015). In this view, patients coordinate information flow, and clinicians are invited by the patients in their healthcare experience and decision-making process. This centricity goes beyond a simple interaction since it embraces the whole patients' health journey, including preferences, values, and beliefs.

Figure 6.1 illustrates the shift from the narrow perspective of patient-centeredness to the broader vision of patient centricity.

Patient centricity is defined as putting the patients first in an open and sustained engagement to provide a high-value experience and outcome for them and their related families in a respectful and compassionate way (Yeoman et al., 2017). This definition embeds some pivotal aspects that are following explained: "the open and sustained engagement" implies

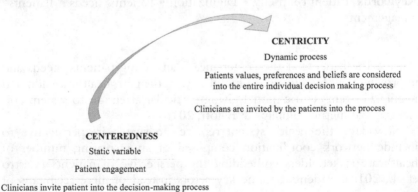

CENTRICITY

Dynamic process

Patients values, preferences and beliefs are considered into the entire individual decision making process

Clinicians are invited by the patients into the process

CENTEREDNESS

Static variable

Patient engagement

Clinicians invite patient into the decision-making process

Fig. 6.1 From centerdness to patient centricity

acting fairly and transparently in all the interactions with patients; the term "respectfully" is linked to a mutual understanding of different stakeholders' perspectives; "compassionately" means be empathic with a person and the related life condition, valorizing patient contribution in healthcare decisions; "achieving the best experience and outcome" implies supporting the person with therapeutic and non-therapeutic means rather than being focused on the patient condition. Aspects of inclusiveness, sharing patient-centric goals, empowering patients, partnership, collaboration, respect, compassion, and openness are comprised in this definition. Stegemann et al. (2016) define patient centricity as the recognition of the needs of an individual patient (including the related physiological, physical, psychological, and social characteristics) comprising their specific needs as the focal point in the overall design of medicine.

In Table 6.1, the main definitions of patient centricity are summarized.

Rethinking the healthcare system with a patient-centric view implies pursuing a process composed of the phases of patient activation, empowerment, involvement, and engagement, as described by Ciasullo et al. (2022). The first phase (activation) concerns the acquired capability of patients to collect health information to increase their awareness on health conditions and to recognize the resources available for health promotion and risk prevention; the second phase (empowerment) concerns the patients' transformation by gaining the knowledge and skills to be involved as co-producers in the provision of healthcare services; the third phase (involvement) activates a continuous dialogue between patients and healthcare professionals, in a perspective of value co-creation; the last phase (engagement) entails healthcare services provision based on a therapeutic alliance between patients and healthcare professionals. Figure 6.2 illustrates these four phases as a path for paving the way to patient centricity.

Service co-production and value co-creation rely on patients' activation, empowerment, involvement, and engagement, which activate a virtuous cycle leading to a durable partnership among patients, caregivers, and healthcare professionals. The relationship between patients and clinicians changes from a reactive approach related to diagnosis and treatment in response to signs and symptoms to a proactive type of health (Schiavone & Ferretti, 2021; Waldman & Terzic, 2019) focused on personalized care based on early warning signals, predictive models, and continuous monitoring of data from different sources (Hamburg & Collins, 2010).

Implementation of patient centricity requires a consistent and coordinated approach, starting from the definition of patients' needs (Hoos

Table 6.1 Patient centricity definitions

Definitions	Authors
Patient centricity is putting the patient first in an open and sustained engagement with the patient to respectfully and compassionately achieve the best experience and outcome for that person and their family	Yeoman et al. (2017)
Patient centricity can be simply defined as integrated measures for listening to and partnering with patients and placing patient wellbeing at the core of all initiatives. In essence, it represents a holistic approach to disease management	Du Plessis et al. (2017)
Patient centricity: the needs of an individual patient or distinct patient populations and their specific needs as the focal point in the overall design of medicine, including the targeted patients' physiological, physical, psychological, and social characteristics	Stegemann et al. (2016)
The antecedents of patient centricity include the individual participation, communication, interdisciplinary teamwork, and a supportive care environment; the attributes include biopsychosocial perspective, the patient as a unique person, a sustainable and genuine patient-care giver relationship; the consequences are knowledge, health behavior, adherence, health outcome, and quality of care.	Castro et al. (2016)
Patient centricity has four core principles: relevance, pragmatism, feasibility, and interactivity	Getz (2015)
There are five most important dimensions of patient centricity: the patient as a unique person, patient involvement in care, patient information, clinician-patient communication, and patient empowerment	Zill et al. (2015)
Patient centricity has 15 interrelated dimensions that can be divided into principles (essential characteristics of the clinician, clinician-patient relationship, patient as a unique person, biopsychosocial perspective), enablers (clinician-patient communication, integration of medical and non-medical care, teamwork and teambuilding, access to care, coordination and continuity of care), and activities (patient information, patient involvement in care, involvement of family and friends, patient empowerment, physical support, emotional support)	Scholl et al. (2014)
Patient centricity is a dynamic process through which the patient regulates the flow of information to and from him/her via multiple pathways to exercise choices consistent with his/her preferences, values, and beliefs	Robbins et al. (2013)
The patient-centered care refers to actions in service of patient-centeredness, including interpersonal behaviors, technical interventions, and health systems innovations	Epstein et al. (2005)
The patient-centered style is a less doctor-controlling model, which encourages patients' participation to foster a mutual relationship	Stewart et al. (2003)

(*continued*)

Table 6.1 (continued)

Definitions	Authors
Patient-centered care is not only a quality of an individual practitioner but also of the health system as a whole	Committee on Quality of Health Care in America (2001)
Patient centricity has five key dimensions: biopsychosocial perspective, the patient-as-person, therapeutic alliance, sharing power and responsibility, and the doctor-as-person	Mead and Bower (2000)
Patient centricity includes six interconnecting components: the disease and illness experience, the whole person, common ground, prevention and health promotion, the doctor-patient relationship, and the availability of time and resources	Brown et al. (1995)
Patient-centered care describes a moral philosophy with three core values: (1) considering patients' needs, wants, perspectives, and individual experiences; (2) offering patients opportunities to provide input into and participate in their care; and (3) enhancing partnership and understanding in the patient-physician relationship	McWhinney (1993)

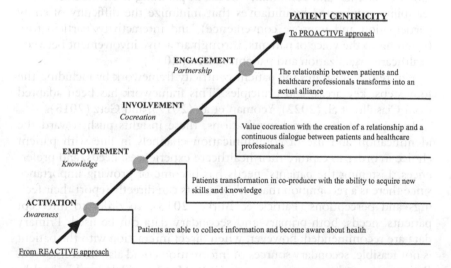

Fig. 6.2 The four phases for achieving patient centricity

et al., 2015) that also includes the comparison between benefit and risk based on their values, their desired clinical outcomes, preferences, and experiences (Yeoman et al., 2017); thus, information has to be accessible to all patients to make them active participants in the decision-making process.

To acquire an overall comprehension of the patient centricity concept, the four steps can be observed along with the four identified key areas evaluated as important to patients on the basis of Yeoman et al.'s (2017) contribution and the four principles derived from Getz's (2015) research. The four key areas of patient centricity are education and information, co-creation, access, and transparency. A patient-centric view implies that information is both accessible and easily understandable. However, based on that research, patients declare that the amount of information they can access is conflicting. Patients need to become knowledgeable by guaranteeing them support for their decisions about health.

The core principles in planning patient centricity are: relevance (aimed at identifying desired needs based on patient input), pragmatism (accommodate patients' and community needs in planning healthcare services), feasibility (supported by initiatives that minimize the difficulty of study participation and improve convenience), and interactivity/participatory (listening to the voice of patients, through an active involvement between healthcare organization and patients) (Getz, 2015).

Figure 6.3 illustrates the patient centricity framework by including the four steps, key areas, and principles. This framework has been adapted from Ciasullo et al. (2022), Yeoman et al. (2017), and Getz (2015).

In terms of managerial implications, these insights push toward the identification and use of communication channels in line with patient choice in order to capture their healthcare experiences, needs, and preferences. Listening the patients' needs has become of growing importance since there is a recognition that only patients can directly report their feelings and perceptions (Patrick & Burke, 2013). In order to intercept patients' needs, both primary and secondary data can be used. Primary data are recommended; however, when direct interaction with the patient is not feasible, secondary sources of information could also be considered. Patient-reported outcome measures (PROMs) are widely used in healthcare in terms of primary data. The purpose is to create a shared decision-making process in which information about patients' preferences and clinical decisions (i.e., treatments, goals of care, and supportive services) are collected (Sawatzky et al., 2021; Elwyn et al., 2014). It has to be noted

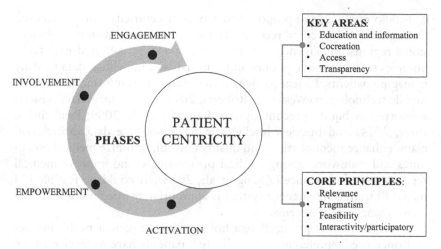

Fig. 6.3   Framework of patient centricity: four steps, key areas, and principles

that needs/preferences can vary based of the specific stage of care; thus, it is relevant that goal setting is always aligned to the patient's current priorities. Indeed, in the case of a chronic condition, patients need to be supported in the process of adaptation toward new values (Reuben & Jennings, 2019; Miner et al., 2015; Nolte et al., 2013).

A continuous collection, monitoring, and interpretation of patients' standpoints are necessary for establishing a constructive dialogue between patients and clinicians (Mejdahl et al., 2018). Initiatives focused on patient centricity are represented by the possibility of meeting with individuals or groups of patients to identify patients' desired outcomes during treatment: patient advisory boards, professional panels, direct-to-patient clinical trials, home nursing networks, social media analysis (Lamberti & Awatin, 2017). Moreover, a system-wide approach should be applied to empower patients by creating and providing self-management tools of health services through new technologies.

On this purpose, innovation provides great insights into transforming healthcare toward a patient-centric view. Indeed, advances in technology—that is, telemedicine, sensors, wearable solutions, innovative devices, and cloud technologies (see Chap. 1), can optimize patient centricity (Yaakov et al., 2021).

Sebillo et al. (2015) proposed that patient centricity can be achieved through the daily medical records of patients combined with multidimensional regional intelligence systems; the data can be collected with technologies such as mobile phones and sensor-based individual data by daily managing patients. Patient participation is enabled via informatization and mobile technologies (Weston & Roberts, 2013) with managerial decisions supported by big data technologies (McCarthy et al., 2009; Paulheim & Bizer, 2014) and business intelligence to personalize data formulation plans, enhance medical safety and quality control, optimize medical procedures and teamwork among medical professionals, and improve medical services and performance (Zheng et al., 2018). It could be feasible if a medical business intelligence system is appropriately integrated with hospitals' management systems.

From the patient perspective, a holistic view of patient health implies that once needs/preferences are collected, patients have to receive all the required information for optimizing the decision-making process; at this step, technology is crucial for monitoring and supporting care with twofold real-time information: clinical outcomes and patients' needs alignment.

ICT's role is to empower patients and involve them in healthcare provision with technologies such as online patient portals, telemedicine applications, e-healthcare, and mobile health solutions (Ciasullo et al., 2021). In this way, patients' experience with healthcare services can be recorded and personal health data guarantee a continuum of care (Rozenblum et al., 2017). Hence, innovation and patient centricity are strongly intertwined since digitalization is crucial for supporting the activation, empowerment, involvement, and engagement of patients.

Bringing patient centricity into action requires, at first, a vision shared by all stakeholders, and the main steps that should be followed for its implementation at system level are (du Plessis et al., 2017) enabling a change of mindset toward a patient-centric vision, collaborating and involving the entire healthcare network of stakeholders to develop patient-centric solutions, and sharing the learning and experiences in order to transfer the knowledge for the benefit of the system and the community. Moreover, it means to recognize the role of patients and caregivers in service design, health promotion, and risk prevention activities. As a consequence, in order to enable this change, the system has to guarantee access to adequate and timely information in an open and integrated approach finalized at value co-creation and partnership (Ciasullo et al., 2021).

Digital technologies also allow patients to monitor the evolution of their health status and collaborate with healthcare professionals to customize care and treatment based on the achieved health outcomes (Fischer et al., 2020). Indeed, patient empowerment is enabled by enhancing health knowledge and skills, improving self-efficacy and participation in decision-making processes (Markwart et al., 2020).

Patient centricity emerged as part of a global movement of healthcare reform beginning in the early twenty-first century. A growing amount of studies demonstrates that patients who experienced better outcomes are actively engaged in their healthcare (Crouthamel & Mudambi, 2019). Following the patient-centric approach, the entire patient experience can be designed and maximized considering all the interactions between the patients and the providers since they affect patient activities and value creation in healthcare services (Lee, 2019).

The next chapter deals with patient experience definition and mapping.

REFERENCES

Adinolfi, P., Starace, F., & Palumbo, R. (2016). Health outcomes and patient empowerment: The case of health budgets in Italy. *Journal of Health Management, 18*(1), 117–133.

Brown, J., Stewart, M., & Tessier, S. (1995). *Assessing communication between patients and doctors: A manual for scoring patient-centred communication.* Thames Valley Family Practice Research Unit.

Castro, E. M., Van Regenmortel, T., Vanhaecht, K., Sermeus, W., & Van Hecke, A. (2016). Patient empowerment, patient participation and patient-centeredness in hospital care: A concept analysis based on a literature review. *Patient Education and Counseling, 99*(12), 1923–1939.

Ciasullo, M. V., Carli, M., Lim, W. M., & Palumbo, R. (2021). An open innovation approach to co-produce scientific knowledge: An examination of citizen science in the healthcare ecosystem. *European Journal of Innovation Management, 25*, 365.

Ciasullo, M. V., Orciuoli, F., Douglas, A., & Palumbo, R. (2022). Putting health 4.0 at the service of society 5.0: Exploratory insights from a pilot study. *Socio-Economic Planning Sciences, 80*, 101163.

Committee on Quality of Health Care in America, I. o. M. (2001). *Crossing the quality chasm: A new health system for the 21st century.* National Academy Press.

Crouthamel, M., & Mudambi, S. (2019). *The rise of patient centricity in the pharmaceutical industry* (doctoral dissertation, Temple University Libraries).

du Plessis, D., Sake, J. K., Halling, K., Morgan, J., Georgieva, A., & Bertelsen, N. (2017). Patient centricity and pharmaceutical companies: Is it feasible? *Therapeutic Innovation & Regulatory Science, 51*(4), 460–467.

Elwyn, G., Dehlendorf, C., Epstein, R. M., Marrin, K., White, J., & Frosch, D. L. (2014). Shared decision making and motivational interviewing: Achieving patient-centered care across the spectrum of health care problems. *Annals of Family Medicine, 12*(3), 270–275.

Epstein, R. M., Franks, P., Shields, C. G., Meldrum, S. C., Miller, K. N., Campbell, T. L., & Fiscella, K. (2005). Patient centered communication and diagnostic testing. *Annals of Family Medicine, 3*, 415.

Fischer, G., Lundin, J., & Lindberg, J. O. (2020). Rethinking and reinventing learning, education and collaboration in the digital age—From creating technologies to transforming cultures. *International Journal of Information and Learning Technology, 37*(5), 241–252.

Getz, K. A. (2015). Establishing return-on-investment expectations for patient-centric initiatives. *Therapeutic Innovation & Regulatory Science, 49*(5), 745–749.

Hamburg, M. A., & Collins, F. S. (2010). The path to personalized medicine. *The New England Journal of Medicine, 363*(4), 301–304.

Hoos, A., Anderson, J., Boutin, M., Dewulf, L., Geissler, J., Johnston, G., et al. (2015). Partnering with patients in the development and lifecycle of medicines: A call for action. *Therapeutic Innovation & Regulatory Science, 49*(6), 929–939.

Lamberti, M. J., & Awatin, J. (2017). Mapping the landscape of patient-centric activities within clinical research. *Clinical Therapeutics, 39*(11), 2196–2202.

Lee, D. (2019). A model for designing healthcare service based on the patient experience. *International Journal of Healthcare Management, 12*(3), 180–188.

Markwart, H., Bomba, F., Menrath, I., Brenk-Franz, K., Ernst, G., Thyen, U., et al. (2020). Assessing empowerment as multidimensional outcome of a patient education program for adolescents with chronic conditions: A latent difference score model. *PLoS One, 15*(4), e0230659.

McCarthy, D., Mueller, K., & Wrenn, J. (2009). *Mayo Clinic: Multidisciplinary teamwork, physician-led governance, and patient-centered culture drive world-class health care.* Commonwealth Fund.

McWhinney, I. R. (1993). Why we need a new clinical method. *Scandinavian Journal of Primary Health Care, 11*(1), 3–7.

Mead, N., & Bower, P. (2000). Patient-centredness: A conceptual framework and review of the empirical literature. *Social Science & Medicine, 51*(7), 1087–1110.

Mejdahl, C. T., Schougaard, L. M. V., Hjollund, N. H., Riiskjær, E., Thorne, S., & Lomborg, K. (2018). PRO-based follow-up as a means of self-management support—An interpretive description of the patient perspective. *Journal of Patient-Reported Outcomes.* https://doi.org/10.1186/s41687-018-0067-0

Miner, A. S., Schueller, S. M., Lattie, E. G., & Mohr, D. C. (2015). Creation and validation of the cognitive and behavioral response to stress scale in a depression trial. *Psychiatry Research, 230*(3), 819–825. https://doi.org/10.1016/j. psychres.2015.10.033

Nolte, S., Elsworth, G. R., Newman, S., & Osborne, R. H. (2013). Measurement issues in the evaluation of chronic disease self-management programs. *Quality of Life Research, 22*(7), 1655–1664. https://doi.org/10.1007/ s11136-012-0317-1

Patrick, D. L., & Burke, L. (2013). Focusing on the patient in drug development and research. *ISPOR Connections, 19*(6), 5–8.

Paulheim, H., & Bizer, C. (2014). Improving the quality of linked data using statistical distributions. *International Journal on Semantic Web and Information Systems (IJSWIS), 10*(2), 63–86.

Phillips, G., & Elliott, J. (2018). *The path to patient centricity closing the 'how' gap.* IPSOS.

Reuben, D. B., & Jennings, L. A. (2019). Putting goal-oriented patient care into practice. *Journal of the American Geriatrics Society, 67*(7), 1342–1344. https:// doi.org/10.1111/jgs.15885

Robbins, D. A., Curro, F. A., & Fox, C. H. (2013). Defining patient-centricity: Opportunities, challenges, and implications for clinical care and research. *Therapeutic Innovation & Regulatory Science, 47*(3), 349–355.

Rozenblum, R., Greaves, F.; & Bates, D. W. (2017). The role of social media around patient experience and engagement. *BMJ Quality & Safety, 26*(10), 845–848.

Sawatzky, R., Kwon, J. Y., Barclay, R., Chauhan, C., Frank, L., van den Hout, W. B., et al. (2021). Implications of response shift for micro-, meso-, and macro-level healthcare decision-making using results of patient-reported outcome measures. *Quality of Life Research, 30*(12), 3343–3357.

Schiavone, F., & Ferretti, M. (2021). The FutureS of healthcare. *Futures, 134,* 102849.

Scholl, I., Zill, J. M., Härter, M., & Dirmaier, J. (2014). An integrative model of patient-centeredness—A systematic review and concept analysis. *PLoS One, 9*(9), e107828.

Sebillo, M., Tortora, G., Tucci, M., Vitiello, G., Ginige, A., & Di Giovanni, P. (2015). Combining personal diaries with territorial intelligence to empower diabetic patients. *Journal of Visual Languages and Computing, 29,* 1–14.

Stegemann, S., Ternik, R. L., Onder, G., Khan, M. A., & van Riet-Nales, D. A. (2016). Defining patient centric pharmaceutical drug product design. *The AAPS Journal, 18*(5), 1047–1055.

Stewart, M., Brown, J., Weston, W., McWhinney, I., & McWilliam, C. (2003). *Patient-centered medicine-transforming the clinical method.* Radcliffe Medical Press.

Waldman, S. A., & Terzic, A. (2019). Healthcare evolves from reactive to proactive. *Clinical Pharmacology and Therapeutics, 105*(1), 10.

Weston, M., & Roberts, D. W. (2013). The influence of quality improvement efforts on patient outcomes and nursing work: A perspective from chief nursing officers at three large health systems. *Online Journal of Issues in Nursing, 18*(3), e12.

Yaakov, R. A., Güler, Ö., Mayhugh, T., & Serena, T. E. (2021). Enhancing patient centricity and advancing innovation in clinical research with virtual randomized clinical trials (vRCTs). *Diagnostics, 11*(2), 151.

Yeoman, G., Furlong, P., Seres, M., Binder, H., Chung, H., Garzya, V., & Jones, R. R. (2017). Defining patient centricity with patients for patients and caregivers: A collaborative endeavour. *BMJ Innovations, 3*(2), 76.

Zheng, W., Wu, Y. C. J., & Chen, L. (2018). Business intelligence for patient-centeredness: A systematic review. *Telematics and Informatics, 35*(4), 665–676.

Zill, J. M., Scholl, I., Härter, M., & Dirmaier, J. (2015). Which dimensions of patient-centeredness matter?-results of a web-based expert Delphi survey. *PLoS One, 10*(11), e0141978.

CHAPTER 7

Patient Experience

Abstract Patients' experience is linked to the pursuit of patient centricity, and it is central to redesigning the healthcare service delivery around the actual needs of patients. Patient experience is a multidimensional construct composed of subjective and objective elements, and the overall measurement combines the perceived quality of service and descriptions of care.

Since many benefits are associated with a positive patient experience, exploring and mapping the patient journey is helpful to improve healthcare organizations' performance and to manage low-value activities.

The integration of digital health technologies into the patient journey could support healthcare systems to maintain a patient-centric view in two ways: measuring patient experience in real time and contributing to patient engagement.

The chapter sheds light on how to measure patients' experience and depict the patients' journey and touchpoints.

Keywords Patient experience • Patient satisfaction • Patient journey • Journey mapping • Patient journey touchpoints • Continuity of care

Customer experience can be defined as the customer's perception interpretation of the service process and the interactions with it throughout the journey (Johnston & Kong, 2011, p. 8). Providers pay attention to the

M. Toni, G. Mattia, *The Digital Healthcare Revolution*, https://doi.org/10.1007/978-3-031-16340-1_7

operational service quality, which focuses on whether the service is consistent with its predefined specification (Johnston & Kong, 2011), whereas the service quality perceived by the customer is based on their feelings, judgment, interpretation, experience, and perceived benefits (McCarthy et al., 2016).

Patient experience is unique when compared to customer experience in other service sectors. The healthcare context is a people business characterized by a complex emotional context fueled by multiple interactions with physicians in different places. It is a multifaceted care process comprising different emotions (fear, pain, and anxiety) due to diseases or treatments (Kash et al., 2018). Patient experience is integral to the pursuit of patient centricity with a positive association with clinical safety and effectiveness (Doyle et al., 2013), decreased utilization of healthcare services (Bertakis & Azari, 2011), and improved health outcomes (Charmel & Frampton, 2008; Meyer, 2019). Anhang Price et al. (2014) use the term patient experiences to refer to any process observable by patients, including subjective experiences (i.e., level of pain and emotions), objective experiences in terms of measurable aspects (i.e., waiting time), and observations of clinicians' activities and their behavior with patients. Since patient experience has been defined as feedback from patients on what actually happened during the delivery of health services, including both objective and subjective views (Ahmed et al., 2014), two facets are considered: what happens to patients (patients' experiences of care) and how patients report that experience (feedback received about the experiences). On this strength, patient experience consists of two aspects: rational and functional (Doyle et al., 2013). The rational aspect concerns the relation with clinicians in providing health services: their ability to treat patients with respect and compassion, to act in the best interests of the patient, to empower patients through adequate and transparent information, and to engage patients and their family in the decision-making process. The functional aspects are related to healthcare services expectations, such as the provided service itself (effectiveness and efficiency of delivery) and the care environment/facilities (i.e., cleanliness and safety) (McCarthy et al., 2016).

Since the 2000s, the concept of the patient experience has gained importance as health systems move beyond quality and safety targets toward new key performance indicators, including patient satisfaction metrics (Sofaer & Firminger, 2005; Kash et al., 2018). Indeed, patient experience is increasingly recognized as one of the three pillars of quality in healthcare, alongside clinical effectiveness and patient safety (Doyle et al., 2013; Coulter et al., 2009). Policymakers and healthcare organizations strain to collect patient experience data to assess performance and stimulate quality improvement (Ahmed et al., 2014).

Two broad categories of patient-centered care are interrelated: patient experience and satisfaction with care (Larson et al., 2019). These two concepts are often interchangeable, even though they are distinct (Ahmed et al., 2014). Patient experience regards patients' interactions with the health system, whereas patient satisfaction is the evaluation of care provided compared to expectations. Satisfaction is a multidimensional concept influenced by the subjective experiences of patients (Sitzia & Wood, 1997), expectations, preferences for care, and the quality of care received (Staniszewska & Ahmed, 1999; Jackson et al., 2001). The relation between satisfaction and experience is evident by the fact that in some studies, satisfaction has also been conceptualized as one determinant of patient experience (Staniszewska & Ahmed, 1999); vice versa, in other cases, patient experience is considered an element of satisfaction (Bleich et al., 2009). Patient satisfaction is an outcome measure of a patient's experiences of care, health outcomes, and confidence in the health system, reflecting whether or not the care provided has met the patient's needs and expectations (Larson et al., 2019; Kruk et al., 2018).

Also patient experience is a multidimensional construct encompassing several elements of care (Ahmed et al., 2014): the process of making an appointment, cleanliness of facilities, waiting times, the information provided, and interactions with administrative and clinical staff. The English National Health Service (NHS) delineates eight critical aspects to patient experience (Department of Health, 2011): (1) respect for patient-centered values, preferences, and expressed needs; (2) coordination and integration of care across facilities and care system; (3) information, communication, and education to facilitate autonomy, self-care, and health promotion; (4) physical comfort including pain management, help with daily activities, and clean/comfortable surroundings; (5) emotional support and alleviation of fear and anxiety on patients and their families; (6) involvement of family and friends to support patients, accommodating their needs; (7) transition and continuity providing information to support patients' care outside the clinical setting; (8) access to care with particular attention to waiting time.

Patient experience is a process indicator and reflects the interpersonal aspects of the quality of care. It is composed of three domains: effective communication, respect and dignity, and emotional support (Tunçalp et al., 2015; Valentine et al., 2008). However, these domains are directly influenced by the country and health system: facility characteristics (i.e., amount of patients, number of healthcare providers, and availability of services and resources), patients' characteristics (i.e., sociodemographic characteristics, medical condition, clinical history, etc.), type of service (i.e., preventive or non-emergency care versus emergency care). It has to be noted that these modifiers can influence patients' experiences more indirectly by shaping patients' needs, expectations, and values (Larson et al., 2019). Broader social factors, including patient characteristics, such as age and education, can explain variations in patients' experiences of care, ability to evaluate the quality of care received, and satisfaction with care (Bleich et al., 2009). Patient's expectations and interpretations of their experiences of care are further shaped by the broader societal, community, and family contexts (Larson et al., 2019). The overall patient experience combines the perceived quality of service and descriptions of care (Ahmed et al., 2014).

7.1   Measure Patient Experience

Exploring the individual patient journey is helpful to healthcare organizations to improve the patient experience from their perspective instead of the provider one (Halvorsrud et al., 2016; Gualandi et al., 2019).

Kash et al. (2018) propose the Four Ps model of patient experience as a patient-centered framework that can provide healthcare organizations a guide to design and positively influence the patient experience. The four Ps model of patient experience focuses on the people (physicians and partners), processes, and places experienced by patients as part of their journey in receiving medical care. The Four Ps (levers) are divided into physicians; partners (other providers, healthcare employees, and care team staff); places where people interact with physicians and partners; and processes that define and facilitate the clinical care protocol and patient journey. These levers can be adequately managed to build the appropriate workplace culture that facilitates achieving the best patient experiences and satisfaction.

In order to measure whether care is patient-centered, people who have had contact with the healthcare system need to be surveyed (Browne et al., 2010; Anhang Price et al., 2014). Patient-reported data on satisfaction, preferences, outcomes, and experience have been increasingly studied for implementing patient-centered care (Murante et al., 2014; Klose et al., 2016; Gualandi et al., 2021). The patient experience differs compared to patient satisfaction. Patient satisfaction surveys obtain ratings of satisfaction with care, while patient experience surveys extract reports on what patients experienced in their interactions with providers and the healthcare system (Browne et al., 2010). Understanding and assessing patients' experiences and satisfaction requires directly contacting patients, implying a certain level of subjectivity due to self-reports (Larson et al., 2019). Indeed, asking patients a direct report about what happened is less subjective compared to those questions that ask patients to evaluate or rate their experience (Ahmed et al., 2014). Indeed, patient experience is formed during the moments in which the health service and patient meet (McCarthy et al., 2016). Hence, the experience can be measured through several aspects that can also be assessed objectively: waiting time, communication between clinicians and patients, staff responsiveness, availability of information, and cleanliness (Ahmed et al., 2014). The interpersonal aspects such as communication, respect, non-discriminatory treatment, and involvement in decision-making are highly important, whereas patients with long hospitalization give attention to other more tangible aspects such as food and accommodation (Stuart et al., 2003). Effective communication between clinicians and patients can impact health outcomes in terms of emotions, symptom resolution, and functional and physiological measures (Stewart, 1995). Communication positively impacts also patient adherence that is the degree to which patients follow the recommendations of their health professionals (Zolnierek & DiMatteo, 2009).

In order to measure patients' experience, collecting patient data is crucial, and a wide variety of ways and tools can be used on this purpose (Beattie et al., 2015; Coulter et al., 2009). It can be assessed qualitatively or quantitatively (Larson et al., 2019). Qualitative research is useful to explore a patient's values and preferences or to extract new knowledge. Interviews and focus groups can be used to provide more in-depth and descriptive information about a patient's experience with healthcare services (De Silva, 2013). Moreover, qualitative methods can also be used to help validate and enhance information gained from quantitative measures (Larson et al., 2019). Using quantitative validated measures can help researchers address the issue of subjectivity. Survey questionnaires—usually administered on paper—are the preferred method to capture the patient experience and evaluate the quality of healthcare services delivery

(Yanes et al., 2016; Tsianakas et al., 2012). However, questionnaires or traditional collection methods have to adapt to the complexity of patient experience considering the multiple factors embedded in it (Czarniawska, 2007; Gualandi et al., 2019). Time and space dynamics, perceptions, and emotions can occur simultaneously during the experience (Ziebland et al., 2013). The ability to remember the experience (Kjellsson et al., 2014; Icks et al., 2017) and the existence of differences in care across different providers should be considered (Mant, 2001; Larson et al., 2019). Regarding reliability, identifying critical moments in the journey and capturing immediate data is crucial rather than at the end of the experience (Gualandi et al., 2021; Kjellsson et al., 2014). Since the time in which the interview is conducted becomes relevant for data accuracy, using unstructured diaries completed with the patient's own words is often chosen as an adequate option to capture the patient's perspective.

The quantitative tools can be distinguished in patient reports in which they assess what happened and patient evaluations that consist in assigning ratings of their experience (Ahmed et al., 2014). These two approaches can be combined to assess the acceptability of some aspects of care (Bower et al., 2003). In the Picker Institute questionnaire, in order to have a comprehensive view, items have been included along with one final question asking patients to rate the overall care received or whether they recommend the providers to family and friends (Jenkinson et al., 2002; NHS Choices, 2014).

Other sources of feedback on patient experience include comments (complaints and compliments) received by medical staff (Ahmed et al., 2014). It has to be noted that the choice of the data collection method could impact the results: indeed, in some cases, interviews result in reports of negative experiences of care, whereas questionnaires produce positive responses (Ahmed et al., 2014; Tsianakas et al., 2012; Williams et al., 1998).

In order to identify potential areas of improvement in patient experience, a meaningful way of capturing what happens during a care episode is the patient-reported experience measures (PREMs), which is a measure of a patient's experience of the healthcare services. The insights are used for understanding the extent to which specific processes occur, for improving performance and service provision and for measuring progress and outcomes.

The integration of digital health technologies into the patient journey could support healthcare systems to maintain a patient-centric view focused on prevention, early and accurate diagnosis, and treatment adherence. Although there is a digital divide to be managed, the widespread use of mobile phones worldwide creates a fertile ground for active participation in care delivery through home monitoring devices, healthcare apps, wearable technology, and digital health services. Health information technology can support real-time communication, shared decision-making, and information sharing, allowing information to be more readily available and actionable to support quality care (Meyer, 2019). The digital revolution implies transformation in managing, collecting, and storing real-time big data in health information systems. New advancements will affect the continuous improvement of existing processes and the introduction of new ones in line with the necessity to immediately obtain the patient-reported data and make corrections (Gualandi et al., 2021). This evolution will pave the way for personalized medicine that goes beyond the targeted therapy, intending to customize the patient journey on the basis of different patient profiles.

Innovation can have implications on patients' journey in two different ways. At first, new technologies are driving innovative and cost-effective approaches to measuring patient experience in real time with surveys conducted directly to patients through mobile phones, online surveys or portable devices (Ahmed et al., 2014). Second, the digital healthcare revolution contributes to patient engagement, remote monitoring, accurate diagnosis, personalized care, and timely intervention (Devi et al., 2020). Hence, integrating digital technology into each touchpoint of the patient journey represents an opportunity for improving healthcare service delivery by minimizing care interruptions. The next paragraph analyzes in depth the patient journey and its characteristics.

7.2   PATIENT JOURNEY

Understanding the service experience requires the analysis of the customer journey (Gualandi et al., 2021) with all the functional and experiential aspects of service processes from the customer perspective through different touchpoints (Følstad & Kvale, 2018; Kankainen et al., 2012). Describing the patient experience is a complex task since it is shaped before, during, and after interactions with the service provider. The experience in the care context is a multifaceted phenomenon with many aspects contributing to shaping the experience (i.e., health status, the context of care and interaction with different health staff) (Ponsignon et al., 2018; Tax et al., 2013).

In the hospital context, the complexity is due to the necessity to manage patients with different pathologies by integrating multiple actors and services in order to respond quickly to emergencies. Consequently, the patient journey reflects the whole patient experience of care made of successive touchpoints that cross services and different facilities. The assessment of the patient journey allows to identify misalignments between hospital units, wards, and departments.

Providers influence the patient journey by interacting with patients and sharing information (Gualandi et al., 2019). Understanding these interactions can provide relevant insights into patient experience and the related outcomes. The journey map is a tool used to track the healthcare service from the patients' perspective (Trebble et al., 2010; Zomerdijk & Voss, 2009) by depicting the service touchpoints (Bate & Robert, 2006; Bessant & Maher, 2009). The starting point is the patient's awareness of a specific care need and the consequent interaction with the hospital and healthcare professionals (Devi et al., 2020). The patient journey mapping allows viewing the consecutive activities between patients and healthcare systems that shape the patient experience (Trebble et al., 2010; McCarthy et al., 2016) with a visual tool that includes both the physical (functional aspect) and emotional sides (rational aspect) to describe patient behavior, feelings, motivations, and attitudes. Facilities issues, along with managerial and emotional aspects linked to internal and external events, can affect the patient experience (Gualandi et al., 2019; Jain et al., 2017; Plutchik, 1988). By observing the patient journey from the patient perspective, the fragmented care structured in silos increases the complexity due to multiple entry and exit points, considering visits, different departments, and typologies of treatments. Hence, patients may need support during the entire journey of care.

Healthcare is the setting in which patients feel a wide variety of emotions, from powerless and lacking control on their physical/psychological condition and the service process itself. These emotions can impact patient outcomes by inducing passivity, treatment resistance, loneliness, and depression (Berry & Bendapudi, 2007; Berry et al., 2015; Gallan et al., 2013). Other factors that can amplify emotions are personal characteristics (i.e., age, education, socioeconomic status, and income), individual states (i.e., marital status and stress conditions), and contextual factors arising from the environment (accessibility to healthcare facilities and information asymmetry) (Baker et al., 2005). Comprehending the patient journey from the patients' perspective can help healthcare systems evolve their care models to address the patients' needs, increase patients' participation in their health, and improve quality of life (Devi et al., 2020). The patient pathways need to be redesigned based on journey mapping and patients' perspectives, carefully considering each touchpoint in order to inform interventions, improve performance, and eliminate constraints throughout the service experience (McCarthy et al., 2016).

The journey maps illustrate the service delivery interactions in a dynamic way (McCarthy et al., 2016; Zomerdijk & Voss, 2009). These system interactions are composed of various elements: touchpoints, timeline, external influences, internal influences, and barriers, as it has been described by Devi et al. (2020).

- Touchpoints are any point of interaction between a patient and the healthcare system.
- Timeline indicates different amounts of time: each interaction or touchpoint duration, time between touchpoints, and the overall length of the patient journey.
- External influences are any factors beyond the health system's control that stop or slow down the patients' journey.
- Internal influences are any factors that impact the patient journey due to the health system's operations.
- Barriers are any factors that may stop the patient journey such as cost accessibility, time conflicts, patient's emotional state, and socioeconomic pressures.

Since many actors and internal/external influences interact in a patient journey, removing all the potential constraints is essential. The aim is to review influencing factors and recommend strategies to improve patient experience, satisfaction, and outcomes by identifying common touchpoints along the patient journey.

Devi et al. (2020) identify also five broad touchpoints of the patient journey:

1. Awareness of disease and knowledge about associated risk factors: increasing patient activation through health communication strategies improves skills and engagement in healthcare.
2. Screening and risk assessment: screening for risk factors is a cost-effective method for early diagnosis and further prevention of

complications. The provided guidance should be targeted on the type of patient in terms of age and physical condition.

3. Diagnosis and treatment decision: patients and their families have to be considered critical partners in the diagnostic and decision-making processes.

4. Treatment experience and access to care: empowerment results from effective communication in healthcare and determines consequent participation, self-management, positive therapeutic alliance, patient activation, and positive clinical outcomes. Positive results are reinforced when individuals' health needs and preferences are considered in every healthcare decision.

5. Adherence to treatment for long-term management: the adherence rate and health literacy can be supported by frontline community health workers, patient support groups, and innovative e-health technologies.

The examination of these key patient journey touchpoints highlights disease management opportunities and can help prioritize interventions for improving prevention and control. Access to care is also governed by the patient's ability to perceive, seek information, reach, pay, and engage with the healthcare setting (Levesque et al., 2013). Strategies designed for improving the patient journey must consider these factors to ensure a patient-centered perspective.

By analyzing the care journey from the healthcare system perspective with a specific focus on the patients' lens, six sequential stages can be mapped to reveal every facet of interaction between the patient and the health system (Trebble et al., 2010). The phases are subsequent and the process starts with a trigger event characterized by signs or symptoms that are self-assessed by patients ("trigger" phase); then the patient contacts a healthcare facility with specific channels or goes directly to the hospital ("help" phase); the patient's medical condition is assessed ("care" phase), and then on-site or follow-up care follow ("treatment" phase). Based on the results, the patient adapts the lifestyles to reduce readmissions and promote good health ("behavioral change"); the health system fosters engagement between the patient and physician in order to improve communication and quality of life ("proactive care" phase).

Figure 7.1 summarizes the six stages of the care journey and the five related touchpoints.

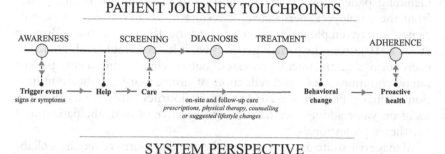

Fig. 7.1   Care journey stages and touchpoints

Patients' experience is increasingly central to assess the performance of healthcare organizations and to redesign the healthcare service delivery around the actual needs of patients (Baig et al., 2020; Kaptain et al., 2019; Specht et al., 2016; Ziebland et al., 2013). Mapping the patient journey is needed to eliminate non-value care activities and waste (Mould et al., 2010; McCarthy et al., 2016).

Several aspects need to be considered in analyzing the patient experience. First, patient journeys are context-specific and rely on national healthcare systems and investments (Devi et al., 2020). Moreover, there are differences on the basis of diseases/treatment and specific needs for individual conditions (Bolz-Johnson et al., 2020). Healthcare organizations should be aware of the populations they serve in order to design a successful patient journey and ensure the best experience for each typology of patient. The patient journey must adopt the patient-centered perspective at each touchpoint of their journey with effective communication strategies for promoting health literacy, patient activation, and awareness (Devi et al., 2020). The patient-centric view is consistent with the fact that the patient is the unique actor who experiences each step of the entire journey (Gualandi et al., 2019). For this reason, hospitals have to invest in exploring and understanding the individual patient journey to improve service quality (Trbovich & Vincent, 2019; Ben-Tovim et al., 2008).

Especially in the case of chronic conditions, healthcare providers need the commitment and action from patients to achieve positive health outcomes (Browne et al., 2010). Patient experience has numerous positive implications. It is positively correlated with key financial indicators, including patient loyalty and retention and reduction of medical risks; from the employees' perspective, it results in greater effectiveness, efficiency, safety, employee satisfaction, and turnover reduction (Browne et al., 2010); from the patient perspective, it leads to higher adherence to prevention and treatment processes, better clinical outcomes, patient safety, communication, and reduction of unnecessary healthcare utilization (Anhang Price et al., 2014). Patient journey analysis increases the focus on value adding care from the perspective of both the patient and healthcare professionals.

Managerial strategies to improve the patient journeys require collaborative planning in health communication programs, communication across settings, shared decision-making, therapeutic alliances between the patient and the provider, self-management tools, connection of all participants across the care continuum, and access to care (Devi et al., 2020; Meyer, 2019).

REFERENCES

Ahmed, F., Burt, J., & Roland, M. (2014). Measuring patient experience: Concepts and methods. *The Patient: Patient-Centered Outcomes Research, 7*(3), 235–241.

Anhang Price, R., Elliott, M. N., Zaslavsky, A. M., Hays, R. D., Lehrman, W. G., Rybowski, L., et al. (2014). Examining the role of patient experience surveys in measuring health care quality. *Medical Care Research and Review, 71*(5), 522–554.

Baig, A., Hall, B., Jenkins, P., Lamarre, E., & McCarthy, B. (2020). *The COVID-19 recovery will be digital: A plan for the first 90 days.* McKinsey & Digital.

Baker, S. M., Gentry, J. W., & Rittenburg, T. L. (2005). Building understanding of the domain of consumer vulnerability. *Journal of Macromarketing, 25*(2), 128–139.

Bate, P., & Robert, G. (2006). Experience-based design: From redesigning the system around the patient to co-designing services with the patient. *BMJ Quality & Safety, 15*(5), 307–310.

Beattie, M., Murphy, D. J., Atherton, I., & Lauder, W. (2015). Instruments to measure patient experience of healthcare quality in hospitals: A systematic review. *Systematic Reviews, 4*(1), 1–21.

Ben-Tovim, D. I., Dougherty, M. L., O'Connell, T. J., & McGrath, K. M. (2008). Patient journeys: The process of clinical redesign. *Medical Journal of Australia, 188*(S6), S14–S17.

Berry, L. L., & Bendapudi, N. (2007). Health care: A fertile field for service research. *Journal of Service Research, 10*(2), 111–122.

Berry, L. L., Davis, S. W., & Wilmet, J. (2015). When the customer is stressed. *Harvard Business Review, 93*(10), 86–94.

Bertakis, K. D., & Azari, R. (2011). Patient-centered care is associated with decreased health care utilization. *Journal of the American Board of Family Medicine, 24*(3), 229–239.

Bessant, J., & Maher, L. (2009). Developing radical service innovations in health-care—The role of design methods. *International Journal of Innovation Management, 13*, 555–568.

Bleich, S. N., Özaltin, E., & Murray, C. J. (2009). How does satisfaction with the health-care system relate to patient experience? *Bulletin of the World Health Organization, 87*(4), 271–278.

Bolz-Johnson, M., Meek, J., & Hoogerbrugge, N. (2020). Patient journeys: Improving care by patient involvement. *European Journal of Human Genetics, 28*(2), 141–143.

Bower, P., Roland, M., Campbell, J., & Mead, N. (2003). Setting standards based on patients' views on access and continuity: Secondary analysis of data from the general practice assessment survey. *BMJ, 326*(7383), 258.

Browne, K., Roseman, D., Shaller, D., & Edgman-Levitan, S. (2010). Measuring patient experience as a strategy for improving primary care. *Health Affairs, 29*(5), 921–925.

Charmel, P. A., & Frampton, S. B. (2008). Building the business case for patient-centered care: Patient-centered care has the potential to reduce adverse events, malpractice claims, and operating costs while improving market share. *Healthcare Financial Management, 62*(3), 80–86.

Coulter, A., Fitzpatrick, R., & Cornwell, J. (2009). *Measures of patients' experience in hospital: Purpose, methods and uses* (pp. 7–9). King's Fund.

Czarniawska, B. (2007). *Shadowing: And other techniques for doing fieldwork in modern societies.* Copenhagen Business School Press DK.

De Silva, D. (2013). *Measuring patient experience* (p. 20). The Health Foundation.

Department of Health. (2011). NHS Patient Experience Framework, NHS National Quality Board (NQB).

Devi, R., Kanitkar, K., Narendhar, R., Sehmi, K., & Subramaniam, K. (2020). A narrative review of the patient journey through the lens of non-communicable diseases in low-and middle-income countries. *Advances in Therapy, 37*(12), 4808–4830.

Doyle, C., Lennox, L., & Bell, D. (2013). A systematic review of evidence on the links between patient experience and clinical safety and effectiveness. *BMJ Open, 3*(1), e001570.

Følstad, A., & Kvale, K. (2018). Customer journeys: A systematic literature review. *Journal of Service Theory and Practice, 28*, 196.

Gallan, A. S., Jarvis, C. B., Brown, S. W., & Bitner, M. J. (2013). Customer positivity and participation in services: An empirical test in a health care context. *Journal of the Academy of Marketing Science, 41*(3), 338–356.

Gualandi, R., Masella, C., Piredda, M., Ercoli, M., & Tartaglini, D. (2021). What does the patient have to say? Valuing the patient experience to improve the patient journey. *BMC Health Services Research, 21*(1), 1–12.

Gualandi, R., Masella, C., Viglione, D., & Tartaglini, D. (2019). Exploring the hospital patient journey: What does the patient experience? *PLoS One, 14*(12), e0224899.

Halvorsrud, R., Kvale, K., & Følstad, A. (2016). Improving service quality through customer journey analysis. *Journal of Service Theory and Practice, 26,* 840.

Icks, A., Dittrich, A., Brüne, M., Kuss, O., Hoyer, A., Haastert, B., et al. (2017). Agreement found between self-reported and health insurance data on physician visits comparing different recall lengths. *Journal of Clinical Epidemiology, 82,* 167–172.

Jackson, J. L., Chamberlin, J., & Kroenke, K. (2001). Predictors of patient satisfaction. *Social Science & Medicine, 52*(4), 609–620.

Jain, R., Aagja, J., & Bagdare, S. (2017). Customer experience – A review and research agenda. *Journal of Service Theory and Practice, 27,* 642.

Jenkinson, C., Coulter, A., Bruster, S., Richards, N., & Chandola, T. (2002). Patients' experiences and satisfaction with health care: Results of a questionnaire study of specific aspects of care. *Quality and Safety in Health Care, 11*(4), 335–339.

Johnston, R., & Kong, X. (2011). The customer experience: A road-map for improvement. *Managing Service Quality: An International Journal, 21,* 5–24.

Kankainen, A., Vaajakallio, K., Kantola, V., & Mattelmäki, T. (2012). Storytelling Group – A co-design method for service design. *Behaviour & Information Technology, 31*(3), 221–230.

Kaptain, K., Ulsøe, M. L., & Dreyer, P. (2019). Surgical perioperative pathways—Patient experiences of unmet needs show that a person-centred approach is needed. *Journal of Clinical Nursing, 28*(11–12), 2214–2224.

Kash, B. A., McKahan, M., Tomaszewski, L., & McMaughan, D. (2018). The four Ps of patient experience: A new strategic framework informed by theory and practice. *Health Marketing Quarterly, 35*(4), 313–325.

Kjellsson, G., Clarke, P., & Gerdtham, U. G. (2014). Forgetting to remember or remembering to forget: A study of the recall period length in health care survey questions. *Journal of Health Economics, 35,* 34–46.

Klose, K., Kreimeier, S., Tangermann, U., Aumann, I., & Damm, K. (2016). Patient-and person-reports on healthcare: Preferences, outcomes, experiences, and satisfaction – An essay. *Health Economics Review, 6*(1), 1–11.

Kruk, M. E., Gage, A. D., Arsenault, C., Jordan, K., Leslie, H. H., Roder-DeWan, S., et al. (2018). High-quality health systems in the sustainable development goals era: Time for a revolution. *The Lancet Global Health, 6*(11), e1196–e1252.

Larson, E., Sharma, J., Bohren, M. A., & Tunçalp, Ö. (2019). When the patient is the expert: Measuring patient experience and satisfaction with care. *Bulletin of the World Health Organization, 97*(8), 563.

Levesque, J. F., Harris, M. F., & Russell, G. (2013). Patient-centred access to health care: conceptualising access at the interface of health systems and populations. *International journal for equity in health, 12*(1), 1–9.

Mant, J. (2001). Process versus outcome indicators in the assessment of quality of health care. *International Journal for Quality in Health Care, 13*(6), 475–480.

McCarthy, S., O'Raghallaigh, P., Woodworth, S., Lim, Y. L., Kenny, L. C., & Adam, F. (2016). An integrated patient journey mapping tool for embedding quality in healthcare service reform. *Journal of Decision Systems, 25*(sup1), 354–368.

Meyer, M. A. (2019). Mapping the patient journey across the continuum: Lessons learned from one patient's experience. *Journal of Patient Experience, 6*(2), 103–107.

Mould, G., Bowers, J., & Ghattas, M. (2010). The evolution of the pathway and its role in improving patient care. *Quality and Safety in Health Care, 19*(5), e14.

Murante, A. M., Seghieri, C., Brown, A., & Nuti, S. (2014). How do hospitalization experience and institutional characteristics influence inpatient satisfaction? A multilevel approach. *The International Journal of Health Planning and Management, 29*(3), e247–e260.

NHS Choices. The NHS friends and family test. 2014.

Plutchik, R. (1988). The nature of emotions: Clinical implications. In *Emotions and psychopathology* (pp. 1–20). Springer.

Ponsignon, F., Smart, A., & Phillips, L. (2018). A customer journey perspective on service delivery system design: Insights from healthcare. *International Journal of Quality & Reliability Management, 35*, 2328.

Sitzia, J., & Wood, N. (1997). Patient satisfaction: A review of issues and concepts. *Social Science & Medicine, 45*(12), 1829–1843.

Sofaer, S., & Firminger, K. (2005). Patient perceptions of the quality of health services. *Annual Review of Public Health, 26*, 513.

Specht, K., Kjaersgaard-Andersen, P., & Pedersen, B. D. (2016). Patient experience in fast-track hip and knee arthroplasty – A qualitative study. *Journal of Clinical Nursing, 25*(5–6), 836–845.

Staniszewska, S., & Ahmed, L. (1999). The concepts of expectation and satisfaction: Do they capture the way patients evaluate their care? *Journal of Advanced Nursing, 29*(2), 364–372.

Stewart, M. A. (1995). Effective physician-patient communication and health outcomes: A review. *CMAJ: Canadian Medical Association Journal, 152*(9), 1423.

Stuart, P. J., Parker, S., & Rogers, M. (2003). Giving a voice to the community: A qualitative study of consumer expectations for the emergency department. *Emergency Medicine, 15*(4), 369–374.

Tax, S. S., McCutcheon, D., & Wilkinson, I. F. (2013). The service delivery network (SDN) a customer-centric perspective of the customer journey. *Journal of Service Research, 16*(4), 454–470.

Trbovich, P., & Vincent, C. (2019). From incident reporting to the analysis of the patient journey. *BMJ Quality & Safety, 28*(3), 169–171.

Trebble, T. M., Hansi, N., Hydes, T., Smith, M. A., & Baker, M. (2010). Process mapping the patient journey: An introduction. *BMJ, 341*, c4078.

Tsianakas, V., Maben, J., Wiseman, T., Robert, G., Richardson, A., Madden, P., et al. (2012). Using patients' experiences to identify priorities for quality improvement in breast cancer care: Patient narratives, surveys or both? *BMC Health Services Research, 12*(1), 1–11.

Tunçalp, Ö., Were, W. M., MacLennan, C., Oladapo, O. T., Gülmezoglu, A. M., Bahl, R., et al. (2015). Quality of care for pregnant women and newborns— The WHO vision. *BJOG, 122*(8), 1045.

Valentine, N., Darby, C., & Bonsel, G. J. (2008). Which aspects of non-clinical quality of care are most important? Results from WHO's general population surveys of "health systems responsiveness" in 41 countries. *Social Science & Medicine, 66*(9), 1939–1950.

Williams, B., Coyle, J., & Healy, D. (1998). The meaning of patient satisfaction: An explanation of high reported levels. *Social Science & Medicine, 47*(9), 1351–1359.

Yanes, A. F., McElroy, L. M., Abecassis, Z. A., Holl, J., Woods, D., & Ladner, D. P. (2016). Observation for assessment of clinician performance: A narrative review. *BMJ Quality & Safety, 25*(1), 46–55.

Ziebland, S., Coulter, A., Calabrese, J. D., & Locock, L. (Eds.). (2013). *Understanding and using health experiences: Improving patient care.* Oxford University Press.

Zolnierek, K. B. H., & DiMatteo, M. R. (2009). Physician communication and patient adherence to treatment: A meta-analysis. *Medical Care, 47*(8), 826.

Zomerdijk, L. G., & Voss, C. A. (2009). Service design for experience-centric services. *Journal of Service Research, 13*, 67–82.

CHAPTER 8

Patient Wellbeing, TSR, and Agenda 2030

Abstract The intrinsic aim of delivering healthcare service is strictly related to patients' wellbeing and quality of life. As the Transformative Service Research (TSR) suggests, successful interaction among several entities and users is crucial to realize wellbeing outcomes, such as access, literacy, decreasing disparity, and enhancing health and happiness.

In the healthcare setting, value co-creation and physical environment affect psychological, existential, support, and physical components of well-being, including the eudaimonic and hedonic spheres.

Digitization contributes in several ways: intensifying value co-creation activities by creating more opportunities for interactions outside the physical environment; moreover, technologies can reduce the sufferings on human lives and society through prevention, early detection, diagnosis, remote care, telehealth, and real-time communication. The chapter proposes a conceptual framework to enlighten the linkage between wellbeing, value co-creation, and physical environment.

Keywords Wellbeing • Transformative service research • Agenda 2030 • Quality of life

The healthcare sector is one of the most critical service systems considering the relevance of the service provided and the pressure of the continuous flow of demand for health services.

M. Toni, G. Mattia, *The Digital Healthcare Revolution*,
https://doi.org/10.1007/978-3-031-16340-1_8

As observed in the previous chapters, healthcare users' roles have evolved by actively interacting with multiple actors in the service setting to improve quality of life (Virlée et al., 2020; Stein & Ramaseshan, 2016; McColl-Kennedy et al., 2015). The healthcare industry is undergoing revolutionary change toward people-centered health services and patients as active participants or co-creators (World Health Organization, 2016; Danaher & Gallan, 2016).

Sustainability is at the core of the system to assure improved patient recovery rate and wellbeing (Dellinger, 2010; Wittmann, 2010). Indeed, healthcare is at the core of the Agenda 2030 to ensure universal health coverage and access to quality healthcare for promoting physical and mental health, wellbeing, and extending life expectancy for all. The key aspect of health systems is to be person-centered, with all individuals having the right to be treated with dignity and respect (Larson et al., 2019).

Innovative transformation can support reconciling the Agenda 2030 and healthcare transformation for achieving the sustainable development goals with high impacts on infrastructures, therapy improvements and inequalities reduction. Technologies can be useful to reduce human and society sufferings in different ways (He et al., 2021; Salam & Bajaba, 2021). For instance, they can be implemented for prevention, early detection, diagnosis, and real-time communication for effective healthcare system management (Brohi et al., 2020). Remote care or telehealth technologies can facilitate flexibility in the responsiveness of the healthcare system in times of crisis (Jazieh & Kozlakidis, 2020; Anthony, 2021). By going beyond the technology implementation in the strict sense, innovation can support the pursuit of collective value, focusing on information content and boosting intersectoral interconnections in terms of resources and know-how, minimizing waste with the main aim of solidarity and collective wellbeing. The concept of solidarity is at the basis of European healthcare systems by securing universal access to affordable, preventive, curative, and good quality healthcare (Charter of Fundamental Rights of the European Union and the European Pillar of Social Rights). The concept of wellbeing acquires pivotal attention in the Transformative Service Research (TSR) field of study: consumers engage with an array of services and service systems every day, and thus, service experiences significantly affect human wellbeing. Transformative service is a broad term that aims to support individuals and societal wellbeing (Newbutt et al., 2020; Ostrom et al., 2015; Anderson et al., 2013). In TSR, service users' wellbeing is a subjective evaluation of the quality of life (McColl-Kennedy et al.,

2017) that involves health, happiness, and prosperity (Mick et al., 2012). TSR aims to enhance the quality of delivered service by focusing on improving consumer wellbeing (Anderson et al., 2013; Rosenbaum et al., 2011).

In a context such as healthcare, this is particularly relevant since the intrinsic nature of health services is strictly related to patients' wellbeing and the provision of aid in ordinary situations or in times of crisis. In delivering healthcare services, the primary aim is social wellbeing through better quality of life (QOL). QOL is described as the wellbeing and happiness of individuals (Yuan, 2001) and is a subjective construct (Sirgy et al., 2006; Dagger & Sweeney, 2006; Salam & Bajaba, 2021). In the medical literature, the patient's medical outcomes include also the patient QOL (Akter et al., 2013; Dagger & Sweeney, 2006), which generally refers to wellbeing (Virlée et al., 2020). Indeed, patient QOL increases both the effectiveness and efficiency of care provision by reducing hospitalization and mortality rates (Konstam et al., 1996; Stewart et al., 1989). The concept of QoL is particularly relevant for patients with chronic conditions as it focuses on the quality of their daily life, the improvement of which is often seen as a critical objective for the healthcare service system (Virlée et al., 2020; Link et al., 2005; McColl-Kennedy et al., 2012).

QOL is often used interchangeably with wellbeing (Yuan, 2001), and it comprises four components as follows (Virlée et al., 2020; McColl-Kennedy et al., 2012):

- Psychological: feelings related to depression, agitation or worry, sadness, and fear of the future.
- Existential: an individual's beliefs about their life, including the beliefs that life is meaningful and worthwhile, and that goals are achievable; how they feel about themselves; and whether they have a sense of control over their life.
- Support: feeling supported and cared for.
- Physical: the individual's most problematic physical symptoms, such as fatigue, pain, and weakness.

These elements can vary on the basis of the typology of patients (from generic to vulnerable individuals) and health services conduct actions that impact the individual's body or psyche, implying also different types of emotions (Berry and Bendapudi, 2007; Gallan et al., 2013).

In terms of types of wellbeing, there are two facets: the eudaimonic and the hedonic wellbeing. Eudaimonic wellbeing can be applied to individual, collective, and ecosystem levels, and it emphasizes the realization of human potential (Sen, 1999; Ryff, 1989). The dimensions of eudaimonic wellbeing are access, literacy, better decision-making, individual and collective health, decreased disparities in health and wellbeing, consumer involvement, harmony, power, respect, support, and social networks. Hedonic wellbeing regards individual and collective levels, and it is linked to pleasure and happiness (Diener & Lucas, 1999). It reflects subjective wellbeing through life satisfaction, positive affect (i.e., happiness and joy), and the absence of negative affect (i.e., tension, fear, and stress). Applying the TSR field of study to healthcare means achieving value-creating interactions between patients and healthcare professionals. The result of these interactions leads to improved wellbeing and the creation of sustainable environments (Hamed et al., 2017). It has to be noted that similar service offerings may have a different impact on users' wellbeing (Anderson et al., 2013). For instance, wellbeing can depend on the level of effort in integrating resources (Sweeney et al., 2015). Indeed, wellbeing is considered the main outcome that depends on how the service is co-created (Anderson et al., 2013), confirming the crucial role of patient's behavior (Menichetti et al., 2014; Phillips et al., 2014; Verleye et al., 2014). Since value cocreation impacts QOL and wellbeing (McColl-Kennedy et al., 2012), it is important to illustrate the related five co-creation practices styles in healthcare and their relation with QOL components: Team Management, Passive Compliance, Insular Controlling, Partnering, Pragmatic Adaption. The Team Management value co-creation activity is characterized by high level of activities and interactions; it is associated with high overall QOL, since it shows a high positive support and psychological domain, and moderately high positive existential domain. The Passive Compliance represents the contrary of Team Management because it is characterized by low level of activities and interactions, implying a relatively low QOL in terms of psychological, existential, and physical dimensions. The Insular Controlling is characterized by a high level of activities and low number of interactions with relatively low QOL overall, with low positive support and existential domains and moderately negative psychological domain in terms of feeling depressed, worried, and sad). The Partnering is characterized by medium level of activities and medium number of interactions with relatively high levels of QOL, exhibiting high positive in the support domain and moderately high positive existential and psychological domains. The Pragmatic Adaption is characterized by a relatively low level of activities and a high number of interactions, associated with moderate QOL as evidenced by moderately positive to high positive levels in the support and moderately positive in the existential and psychological domains.

Digitization can contribute to intensifying these value co-creation activities by creating more opportunities for interactions outside the physical environment. Since they are linked to QOL domains, improving these value co-creation practices through technologies affects wellbeing.

As Chap. 7 explains, healthcare delivery involves multiple touchpoints, including various stakeholders' interactions: patient-to-patient, patient-to-health professionals, and health professionals-to-health professionals (Salam & Bajaba, 2021). The interaction of healthcare professionals and patients in a cooperative effort to share data about the evolution of the individual health condition contributes to train about behaviors and decisions and to improve their wellbeing. Service users have different skills and abilities to perform the required health activities; thus, service impact on wellbeing should be also examined from the demand side (Hibbert et al., 2012). Patient centricity, with integrated measures for listening to and partnering with patients (du Plessis et al., 2017), is pivotal for achieving wellbeing through a holistic approach to disease management. In a TSR context, it is also highly relevant to consider users' network, which consists, for instance, of friends, family, and other patients that can strongly affect healthcare service users' experiences and preferences (Anderson et al., 2013).

Quality of system, interaction, and information are fundamentals and can transform the entire healthcare system impacting satisfaction and overall QOL (Salam & Bajaba, 2021). Indeed, the relationship between healthcare system quality, service system satisfaction, and perceptions of QOL is well established in the quality literature (Dagger & Sweeney, 2006). On this strength, Lusch et al. (2007) argued that the customer is a primary integrator of resources in creating value through service experiences intertwined with life experiences to enhance life quality (Salam & Bajaba, 2021; Payne et al., 2008).

Technological advancements, such as telemedicine, remote healthcare (i.e., telehealth, digital therapeutics, and care navigation), enhance stakeholders' QOL and opportunities for co-creation by leading to the concept of separability, on the basis of which patients could access care ubiquitously, even outside hospital facilities.

Besides technological assets, the evidence-based design (EBD) research highlights that tangible items in a service setting (Zeithaml et al., 2006; Lovelock & Wright, 2002) contribute improving patients' experience and wellbeing (Hamed et al., 2017). The EBD focuses on utilizing research findings for designing the hospital physical environment (servicescape) to improve patient wellbeing (Ulrich et al., 2010; Henriksen et al., 2007). This research field has received growing attention, indicating the importance of investing in healthcare facilities layout since the servicescape design impacts the wellbeing of patients (Malone & Dellinger, 2011; Ulrich et al., 2008). The servicescape includes several components: the building itself in terms of its interior (from the entrance, to the paths, signage, elevators, stairs, departments/wards, leisure and waiting areas, furniture, and objects) and exterior designs (environments outside the building, such as gardening and landscape, parking area, and signage system) (Zeithaml et al., 2006; Lovelock & Wright, 2002). These interior and exterior designs represent the stimuli that affect the experiences of users (Bitner, 1992). The servicescape is divided into three stimuli groups: ambient conditions, spatial layout and functionality, and signs, symbols, and artifacts (Bitner, 1992). All three groups together constitute the perceived servicescape that customers use as tangible objects to evaluate the service received (Zeithaml et al., 2006). Therefore, it is important to understand the effect of these stimuli on patient wellbeing and sustainability.

The three stimuli can be divided into specific aspects. The spatial layout and functionality is represented by safety and hygiene, and patient single rooms. The ambient conditions are composed of art, visuals, and music; and plants, greenery, and lighting. Signs, symbols, and artifacts are represented by signage and way-finding (Hamed et al., 2017).

The appearance of a hospital shapes the first impression because it is the first point of contact (Fottler et al., 2000; Vilnai-Yavetz & Gilboa, 2010; Whitehead et al., 2007). Patients evaluate the cleanliness of a hospital on the basis of the level of cleanliness of places and objects, and of the behavior of healthcare employees (Whitehead et al., 2007). Hygiene is linked to safety because it reduces the risks of infection.

Patient room reduces the interactions with other patients, increasing the level of patients' satisfaction by improving privacy and reducing risks of infection (Ben-Abraham et al., 2002; Bracco et al., 2007; Chaudhury et al., 2005). This aspect positively impacts on effective patient care, with employees more satisfied and efficient in managing patients' care (Chaudhury et al., 2005). Planning ad hoc spaces for patients, families, and friends improve the patients' wellbeing (Berry et al., 2004; Sadler et al., 2011).

Greenery due to plants or window views reduces the stress of patients and staff (Ulrich, 1984, 2002), resulting in less pain medication and reducing hospital stay. As a consequence, it causes a reduction of hospital costs in terms of occupied beds and electricity expenses. Moreover, exposure to natural sunlight through patient room windows is another important aspect that speeds the recovery process of patients (Benedetti et al., 2001; Beauchemin & Hays, 1996). Full control of lighting and room assets increases relaxation and satisfaction (Trochelman et al., 2012; Berry et al., 2004; Ulrich, 1991).

Art and visuals impact the reputation of a hospital, affecting also the work environment (Todd, 2009). In particular, natural pictures/paintings and music improve the level of relaxation and satisfaction (Ulrich, 1991; Tansik & Routhieaux, 1999).

Signage systems and way-finding allow patients and healthcare professionals to orient themselves in the environment, improving efficiency and productivity, satisfaction, and relaxation (Mollerup, 2009; Sadler et al., 2011). Interior design should be aligned with signage systems appearance and colors (Mollerup, 2009). Accordingly, there should be consistency in the overall design of the hospital's physical environment.

Achieving patient wellbeing and a sustainable healthcare service provision requires focusing on the aspects illustrated in Table 8.1.

In order to enhance wellbeing, TSR focuses on improving the services provided, whereas EBD focuses on designing the hospital's physical environment. The EBD insights on hospital servicescape designs should be combined with TSR to reach one common goal of improved experience and patient wellbeing within hospitals enhancing competitive advantage in terms of improved medical outcomes (Hamed et al., 2017).

Figure 8.1 illustrates the whole framework of patients' wellbeing.

This framework has practical implications for marketers and managers of hospitals as well as contributions to the academic research domain by expanding patients' experience knowledge. It can represent a guideline for developing, building, or redesigning future hospital servicescapes applying the patients' wellbeing lens.

Table 8.1 Serviscape aspects

Spatial layout and functionality

Safety and hygiene	• Hygiene is related to the risk of infection and it is related to the success or failure of the medical service • The appearance of a hospital shapes the first impression and is the first aspect people notice • Cleanliness is evaluated based on: the overall appearance of the hospital and its interior design, how clean the places and physical objects are, and how healthcare employees behave
Patient rooms	• Patient single rooms reduce the risk of infection and increase the level of patient satisfaction • The lower interactions with other patients increase feeling of privacy and leads to higher satisfaction and efficiency by healthcare employees • Having ad hoc spaces for patients, families, and friends improves the patients' wellbeing

Ambient conditions

Plants, greenery, and natural lighting	• Plants and gardens create a healthier environment • Greenery reduces the stress of patients and staff • Rooms with window view, natural sunlight, and greenery speed up the recovery process of patients • A good design of the physical environment with window view and exposure to natural sunlight can reduce hospital costs in terms of occupied beds and electricity expenses • Physical environment with window view has a positive effect on hospital employees • Patients' satisfaction and relaxation is higher if they can control room lighting and assets
Art, visuals, and music	• Art in hospitals impacts the reputation of the hospital and has an effect on the working environment • Pictures/painting of nature have a relaxing effect on patients • Music improves relaxation and patient satisfaction

Signs, symbols, and artifacts

Signage system	• Way-finding inside hospitals is important for both staff and patients in improving efficiency and productivity • Patients orienting their self around a hospital are more satisfied and relaxed • Signs in an environment adds to the attractiveness and good reputation • The interior design of the building should simplify way-finding by harmonizing colors and appearances

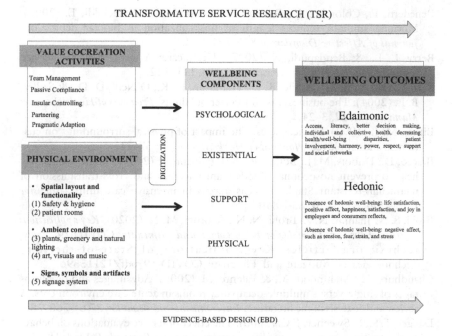

Fig. 8.1 Patients' wellbeing framework

References

Akter, S., D'Ambra, J., Pradeep, R., & Hani, U. (2013). Modelling the impact of mHealth service quality on satisfaction, continuance and quality of life. *Behaviour and Information Technology, 32*(12), 1225–1241.

Anderson, L., Ostrom, A. L., Corus, C., Fisk, R. P., Gallan, A. S., Giraldo, M., et al. (2013). Transformative service research: An agenda for the future. *Journal of Business Research, 66*(8), 1203–1210.

Anthony, B. (2021). Implications of telehealth and digital care solutions during COVID-19 pandemic: A qualitative literature review. *Informatics for Health and Social Care, 46*(1), 68–83.

Beauchemin, K. M., & Hays, P. (1996). Sunny hospital rooms expedite recovery from severe and refractory depressions. *Journal of Affective Disorders, 40*(1–2), 49–51.

Ben-Abraham, R., Keller, N., Szold, O., Vardi, A., Weinberg, M., Barzilay, Z., & Paret, G. (2002). Do isolation rooms reduce the rate of nosocomial infections in the pediatric intensive care unit? *Journal of Critical Care, 17*(3), 176–180.

Benedetti, F., Colombo, C., Barbini, B., Campori, E., & Smeraldi, E. (2001). Morning sunlight reduces length of hospitalization in bipolar depression. *Journal of Affective Disorders, 62*(3), 221–223.

Berry, L. L., & Bendapudi, N. (2007). Healthcare: A fertile field for service research. *Journal of Service Research, 10*(2), 111–122.

Berry, L. L., Parker, D., Coile, R. C., Hamilton, D. K., O'Neill, D. D., & Sadler, B. L. (2004). The business case for better buildings. *Frontiers of Health Services Management, 21*, 3–24.

Bitner, M. J. (1992). Servicescapes: The impact of physical surroundings on customers and employees. *Journal of Marketing, 56*(2), 57–71.

Bracco, D., Dubois, M. J., Bouali, R., & Eggimann, P. (2007). Single rooms may help to prevent nosocomial bloodstream infection and cross-transmission of methicillin-resistant Staphylococcus aureus in intensive care units. *Intensive Care Medicine, 33*(5), 836–840.

Brohi, S. N. Jhanjhi, N. Z. Brohi, N. N., & Brohi, M. N. (2020). *Key applications of state-of-the-art technologies to mitigate and eliminate COVID-19.* www. techrxiv.org/articles/Key_Applications_of_State-of-the-Art_ Technologies_to_Mitigate_and_Eliminate_COVID-19_pdf/12115596

Chaudhury, H., Mahmood, A., & Valente, M. (2005). Advantages and disadvantages of single-versus multiple-occupancy rooms in acute care environments: A review and analysis of the literature. *Environment and Behavior, 37*(6), 760–786.

Dagger, T. S., & Sweeney, J. C. (2006). The effect of service evaluations on behavioral intentions and quality of life. *Journal of Service Research, 9*(1), 3–18.

Danaher, T. S., & Gallan, A. S. (2016). Service research in health care: Positively impacting lives. *Journal of Service Research, 19*(4), 433–437.

Dellinger, B. (2010). Healing environments. In C. S. McCullough (Ed.), *Evidence-based design for healthcare facilities* (pp. 45–79). Sigma Theta Tau International.

Diener, E., & Lucas, R. E. (1999). Personality and subjective well-being. In D. Kahneman, E. Diener, & N. Schwartz (Eds.), *Well-being: The foundations of hedonic psychology* (pp. 213–229). Russell Sage Foundation.

du Plessis, D., Sake, J. K., Halling, K., Morgan, J., Georgieva, A., & Bertelsen, N. (2017). Patient centricity and pharmaceutical companies: Is it feasible? *Therapeutic Innovation & Regulatory Science, 51*(4), 460–467.

Fottler, M. D., Ford, R. C., Roberts, V., & Ford, E. W. (2000). Creating a healing environment: The importance of the service setting in the new consumer-oriented healthcare system. *Journal of Healthcare Management, 45*(2), 91–106.

Gallan, A. S., Jarvis, C. B., Brown, S. W., & Bitner, M. J. (2013). Customer positivity and participation in services: An empirical test in a health care context. *Journal of the Academy of Marketing Science, 41*(3), 338–356.

Hamed, S., El-Bassiouny, N., & Ternes, A. (2017). Evidence-based design and transformative service research application for achieving sustainable healthcare services: A developing country perspective. *Journal of Cleaner Production, 140*, 1885–1892.

He, W., Zhang, Z. J., & Li, W. (2021). Information technology solutions, challenges and suggestions for tackling the COVID-19 pandemic. *International Journal of Information Management, 57,* 102287.

Henriksen, K., Isaacson, S., Sadler, B. L., & Zimring, C. M. (2007). The role of the physical environment in crossing the quality chasm. *The Joint Commission Journal on Quality and Patient Safety, 33*(11), 68–80.

Hibbert, S., Winklhofer, H., & Temerak, M. S. (2012). Customers as resource integrators: Toward a model of customer learning. *Journal of Service Research, 15*(3), 247–261.

Jazieh, A. R., & Kozlakidis, Z. (2020). Healthcare transformation in the post-coronavirus pandemic era. *Frontiers in Medicine, 7,* 429.

Konstam, V., Salem, D., Pouleur, H., Kostis, J., Gorkin, L., Shumaker, S., Mottard, I., Woods, P., Konstam, M. A., & Yusuf, S. (1996). Baseline quality of life as a predictor of mortality and hospitalization in 5,025 patients with congestive heart failure. *The American Journal of Cardiology, 78*(8), 890–895.

Larson, E., Sharma, J., Bohren, M. A., & Tunçalp, Ö. (2019). When the patient is the expert: Measuring patient experience and satisfaction with care. *Bulletin of the World Health Organization, 97*(8), 563.

Link, L. B., Robbins, L., Mancuso, C. A., & Charlson, M. E. (2005). How do cancer patients choose their coping strategies? A qualitative study. *Patient Education and Counseling, 58*(1), 96.

Lovelock, C. H., & Wright, L. K. (2002). *Principles of service marketing and management.* Pearson Education.

Lusch, R. F., Vargo, S. L., & O'brien, M. (2007). Competing through service: Insights from service-dominant logic. *Journal of Retailing, 83*(1), 5–18.

Malone, E. B., & Dellinger, B. A. (2011). *Furniture design features and healthcare outcomes.* The Center for Health Design.

McColl-Kennedy, J. R., Gustafsson, A., Jaakkola, E., Klaus, P., Radnor, Z., Perks, H., & Friman, M. (2015). Fresh perspectives on customer experience. *Journal of Services Marketing, 29*(6/7), 430–435.

McColl-Kennedy, J. R., Hogan, S. J., Witell, L., & Snyder, H. (2017). Cocreative customer practices: Effects of health care customer value cocreation practices on well-being. *Journal of Business Research, 70*(1), 55–66.

McColl-Kennedy, J. R., Vargo, S. L., Dagger, T. S., Sweeney, J. C., & van Kasteren, Y. (2012). Health care customer value cocreation practice styles. *Journal of Service Research, 15*(4), 370–389.

Menichetti, J., Libreri, C., Lozza, E., & Graffigna, G. (2014). Giving patients a starring role in their own care: A bibliometric analysis of the on-going literature debate. *Health Expectations, 19*(3), 516–526.

Mick, D. G., Pettigrew, S., Pechmann, C. C., & Ozanne, J. L. (2012). *Transformative consumer research for personal and collective well-being.* Taylor & Francis Group.

Mollerup, P. (2009). Wayshowing in hospital. *Australasian Medical Journal, 1*(10), 112.

Newbutt, N., Schmidt, M. M., Riva, G., & Schmidt, C. (2020). The possibility and importance of immersive technologies during COVID-19 for autistic people. *Journal of Enabling Technologies, 14*(3), 187–199.

Ostrom, A. L., Parasuraman, A., Bowen, D. E., Patrício, L., & Voss, C. A. (2015). Service research priorities in a rapidly changing context. *Journal of Service Research, 18*(2), 127–159.

Payne, A. F., Storbacka, K., & Frow, P. (2008). Managing the co-creation of value. *Journal of the Academy of Marketing Science, 36*(1), 83–96.

Phillips, R. L., Short, A., Kenning, A., Dugdale, P., Nugus, P., McGowan, R., & Greenfield, D. (2014). Achieving patient-centred care: The potential and challenge of the patient-as-professional role. *Health Expectations, 18*(6), 2616–2628.

Rosenbaum, M., Corus, C., Ostrom, A., Anderson, L., Fisk, R., Gallan, A., Giraldo, M., Mende, M., Mulder, M., Rayburn, S., Shirahada, K., Williams, J. (2011). Conceptualisation and aspirations of transformative service research. *Journal of Research for Consumers.* Pace University Marketing Research Paper No. 2016/03. SSRN. https://ssrn.com/abstract=2643219

Ryff, C. D. (1989). Happiness is everything, or is it? Exploration on the meaning of psychological well-being. *Journal of Personality and Social Psychology, 57*, 1069–1081.

Sadler, B. L., Berry, L. L., Guenther, R., Hamilton, D. K., Hessler, F. A., Merritt, C., & Parker, D. (2011). Fable hospital 2.0: The business case for building better health care facilities. *Hastings Center Report, 41*(1), 13–23.

Salam, M. A., & Bajaba, S. (2021). The role of transformative healthcare technology on quality of life during the COVID-19 pandemic. *Journal of Enabling Technologies, 15*, 87.

Sen, A. (1999). *Development as freedom.* Oxford University Press.

Sirgy, M. J., Lee, D. J., & Bae, J. (2006). Developing a measure of internet well-being: Nomological (predictive) validation. Social Indicators Research, 78(2), 205–249.

Stein, A., & Ramaseshan, B. (2016). Towards the identification of customer experience touch point elements. *Journal of Retailing and Consumer Services, 30*(1), 8–19.

Stewart, A. L., Greenfield, S., Hays, R. D., Wells, K., Rogers, W. H., Berry, S. D., McGlynn, E. A., & Ware, J. E. (1989). Functional status and well-being of patients with chronic conditions: Results from the medical outcomes study. *Journal of the American Medical Association, 262*(7), 907–913.

Sweeney, J. C., Danaher, T. S., & McColl-Kennedy, J. R. (2015). Customer effort in value cocreation activities: Improving quality of life and behavioral intensions of health care customers. *Journal of Service Research, 18*(3), 318–335.

Tansik, D. A., & Routhieaux, R. (1999). Customer stress-relaxation: The impact of music in a hospital waiting room. *International Journal of Service Industry Management, 10,* 68.

Todd, K. (2009). Public art: A case study at Nundah Community Health Centre, Queensland. *Australasian Medical Journal, 1*(10), 115–120.

Trochelman, K., Albert, N., Spence, J., Murray, T., & Slifcak, E. (2012). Patients and their families weigh in on evidence-based hospital design. *Critical Care Nurse, 32*(1), e1–e10.

Ulrich, R. S. (1984). View through a window may influence recovery from surgery. *Science, 224*(4647), 420–421.

Ulrich, R.S. (1991), "Effects ofinterior designonwellness: theoryandrecent scientific research", *Journal of Healthcare Interior Design, 3*(1), 97–109.

Ulrich, R. S. (2002). Health benefits of gardens in hospitals. In *Paper for conference, plants for people International Exhibition Floriade* (Vol. 17, No. 5, p. 2010).

Ulrich, R. S., Berry, L. L., Quan, X., & Parish, J. T. (2010). A conceptual framework for the domain of evidence-based design. *HERD: Health Environments Research & Design Journal, 4*(1), 95–114.

Ulrich, R. S., Zimring, C., Zhu, X., DuBose, J., Seo, H. B., Choi, Y. S., et al. (2008). A review of the research literature on evidence-based healthcare design. *HERD: Health Environments Research & Design Journal, 1*(3), 61–125.

Verleye, K., Gemmel, P., & Rangarajan, D. (2014). Managing engagement behaviors in a network of customers and stakeholders: Evidence from the nursing home sector. *Journal of Service Research, 17*(1), 68–84.

Vilnai-Yavetz, I., & Gilboa, S. (2010). The effect of servicescape cleanliness on customer reactions. *Services Marketing Quarterly, 31*(2), 213–234.

Virlée, J., Van Riel, A. C., & Hammedi, W. (2020). Health literacy and its effects on well-being: How vulnerable healthcare service users integrate online resources. *Journal of Services Marketing, 34*(5), 697–715.

Whitehead, H., May, D., & Agahi, H. (2007). An exploratory study into the factors that influence patients' perceptions of cleanliness in an acute NHS trust hospital. *Journal of Facilities Management, 5,* 275.

Wittmann, M. (2010). Sustainable healthcare design. In C. S. McCullough (Ed.), *Evidence-based design for healthcare facilities* (pp. 147–185). Sigma Theta Tau International.

World Health Organization. (2016). Framework on integrated, people-centred health services. Geneva: World Health Organization, 2019.

Yuan, L. L. (2001). Quality of life case studies for university teaching in sustainable development. *International Journal of Sustainability in Higher Education, 2,* 127–138.

Zeithaml, V. A., Bitner, J., & Gremler, D. D. (2006). *Services marketing: Integrating customer focus across the firm.* McGraw-Hill/Irwin.

CHAPTER 9

Theoretical Framework and Conclusions

Abstract This chapter proposes an overall framework that links the topics discussed in all the previous chapters. The role of digitization in supporting the healthcare revolution toward patient centricity is highlighted by its potential to boost value provided to patients, experience of care, multidirectional collaboration, and patients' wellbeing.

Keywords Theoretical framework • Digital innovation • Sustainability • Value maximization • Patient focus • Digital healthcare revolution

This book originates from the necessity to shed light on the current challenges that healthcare is facing and to propose solutions to overcome them. Worldwide demographic change with increasingly aging populations and the pandemic emergency requires targeted health that considers the difference in health conditions among populations, protecting vulnerable groups.

This chapter provides an overview retracing all the previous chapters by linking the emerged concepts. The aim is to illustrate how each topic is strictly linked with the others and how the digital revolution reinforces these relations.

Digitization offers a tool for projecting healthcare toward a new scenario of flexibility, collaboration, communication, and efficiency in managing

M. Toni, G. Mattia, *The Digital Healthcare Revolution*,
https://doi.org/10.1007/978-3-031-16340-1_9

patients' experience of care. As it has been observed, tackling the challenge of an aging population, implying consequent pressure in health demand, requires moving from a reactive approach to disease to a proactive one based on health and wellbeing. This transformation implies a comprehensive approach that aims at solving more than one challenge simultaneously. Digital innovation covers this role by serving the healthcare system, supporting a multidisciplinary approach based on collaboration, and eliminating barriers due to silos organizations. Interdisciplinary approaches and multidirectional collaboration are pivotal to reducing fragmentation in health delivery and care interruptions. Technological innovation can be a supporting tool in twofold perspectives: increasing the efficiency of the healthcare management system and enhancing patient centricity through communication, access, literacy, engagement, and participation in decision-making. The healthcare revolution through digitization implies a change in the way value is delivered to patients. Patient centricity becomes the main scope of the healthcare system, and it can be achieved by moving the attention from the providers to the patients and rethinking their experience by analyzing each step of the patient's journey, encouraging stakeholders' engagement, value co-creation, and pursuing Value-Based Healthcare. This scenario is feasible with the implementation of digital health accompanied by a systemic and cultural transformation of the expertise of health employees and all the other involved professionals. Thus, the profound impact of disruptive technologies, along with a change in mindset, is expected to shape the future of health systems.

Three themes significantly linked to technological innovation arise from the previous chapters: sustainability, value maximization, and patient focus. These themes represent the scenario in which the digital healthcare revolution is going to occur.

Regarding the first theme, sustainability is at the core of the system to assure improved patient recovery rate and wellbeing. The introduction of One Health, Agenda 2030, and TSR has linked sustainability to healthcare. The One Health concept and its extension from the animal context to sustainable development represents a crucial moment. From that moment onward, the relationship between humans, animals, and the environment became inextricably linked and required a global approach and effort among multiple disciplines to address health for people, animals, and the environment. Advances in digital technology introduce One Digital Health concept, which analyzes the digital health ecosystem by integrating human and veterinary medical data into real-time information systems to support public health. With One Health and One Digital Health, the concept of human health is integrated with wellbeing and sustainability. The Agenda 2030 for Sustainable Development aims to build a global collaboration to address the social challenges that all countries face regarding inequalities. In healthcare, the impact of social inequalities reflects an unfair distribution of resources and health threats. Indeed, effective health services should be able to manage the health of the entire population. The fundamental concept of European healthcare systems is solidarity for securing universal access to affordable, preventive, curative, and high-quality healthcare. The technological implementation supports the pursuit of collective value, focusing on information content and boosting intersectoral interconnections in terms of resources and know-how, minimizing waste with the main aim of solidarity and collective wellbeing. The concept of wellbeing acquires pivotal attention in the TSR field of study based on the assumption that consumers engage with an array of services and service systems every day; thus, service experiences significantly affect human wellbeing. Technologies can be useful to reduce the suffering in human lives and society through prevention, early detection, diagnosis, and real-time communication. Tools like remote care technologies can facilitate flexibility and the healthcare system's capacity to promptly respond to emergency. Moreover, telehealth, digital therapeutics, and care navigation enhance the quality of life by putting into practice the concept of separability, on which patients can easily access care services without going physically to hospital facilities.

The second emerging theme is value maximization. Since the traditional model of care is undergoing radical transformations to face emerging challenges that impact businesses and society, there is a need to switch from "volume of patients" to "value for patients" to pursue Value-Based Healthcare. This approach moves from a fragmented system based on a silos structure to an integrated one focusing on creating value for patients. Technological innovation and collaboration are at the center of interest for ensuring resilience, guaranteeing real-time decision-making and business continuity; by overcoming fragmentation, digital technology presents some benefits for patients in terms of avoiding duplication of care, time, and cost. Moreover, it implies an improvement of patients' value toward a more experiential and systemic value creation setting with multiple actors involved in integrating resources. This transformation implies considering the healthcare service provision through a value co-creation lens. In this scenario, patients act as resource integrators and active co-creators of value in collaboration with healthcare professionals. Hence, it requires a rethought of the health offering with the lens of patient experience and patient centricity. Digital health is a lever for empowering patients by facilitating the exchange with healthcare professionals and minimizing barriers.

The third theme is patient focus, represented by patient centricity and patient experience. Consistently with the previous themes, implementing patient centricity requires a consistent and coordinated approach to make the patients active participants in the decision-making process by identifying their needs and allowing them access to information. Patient-centric technology comes into action by monitoring and supporting care with twofold real-time information: clinical outcomes and patients' needs alignment. Patients are empowered and involved in healthcare provision with technologies such as online patient portals, telemedicine applications, e-healthcare, and mobile health solutions (Ciasullo et al., 2020). In this way, patients' experience with healthcare services can be recorded and personal health data guarantee a continuum of care (Rozenblum et al., 2017). Innovation and patient centricity are strongly intertwined since digitalization is crucial for supporting patients' activation, empowerment, involvement, and engagement of patients.

Patients' experience is linked to the pursuit of patient centricity and is central to redesigning the healthcare service delivery consistent with the actual needs of patients. Integrating digital health technologies into the patient experience could support healthcare systems to maintain a patient-centric view in two ways: measuring patient experience in real time and contributing to patient engagement.

Based on these assumptions, Fig. 9.1 represents the relations between topics and the overall framework.

Table 9.1 shows the three emerging themes and the related topics and indicates how technological innovation contributes to enhance each one.

Digitization boosts all three themes and the effects impact different interrelated levels: patients and healthcare professionals (micro level), healthcare organizations (meso level), and governments and policymakers (macro level). Undertaken actions have multidirectional impacts among different stakeholders and levels of influence.

Bringing a change toward a novel understanding of patient value requires a vision shared by all stakeholders following some steps for its implementation at system level (du Plessis et al., 2017): enabling a change of mindset toward a patient-centric vision; collaborating and involving the entire healthcare network of stakeholders to develop patient-centric

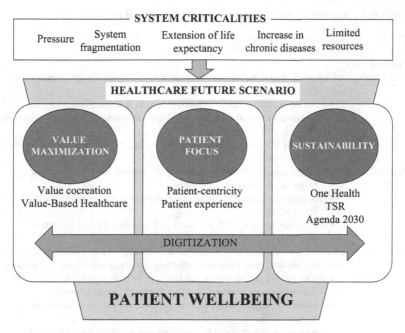

Fig. 9.1 Healthcare digital revolution framework

solutions; sharing the learning and experiences in order to transfer the knowledge for the benefit of the system and the community; recognizing the role of patients and caregivers in service design, health promotion, and risk prevention activities; ensuring access to adequate and timely information in an open and integrated approach finalized at value co-creation and partnership (Ciasullo et al., 2020).

Digital technologies allow to create an open system in which patients can monitor the evolution of their health status and collaborate with healthcare professionals to customize care and treatment based on their needs and achieved health outcomes. Patient empowerment is enabled by investing in health knowledge and skills, improving self-efficacy and participation in decision-making processes (Markwart et al., 2020). Patients' access to timely health information is a requisite for transitioning toward a patient-centric approach to healthcare (Ciasullo et al., 2020).

Table 9.1   Details of themes, topics, and technological implications

Theme	Technological implications

Sustainability

One Health   Advances in digital technology introduce One Digital Health concept that aims at:
- analyzing the digital health ecosystem by integrating human and veterinary medical data into real-time information systems to support public health;
- digitally integrating the concept of human health with wellbeing and sustainability.

Agenda 2030   Technological implementation supports the pursuit of collective value by:
- focusing on information content;
- boosting intersectoral interconnections in terms of resources and know-how;
- minimizing waste with the main aim of solidarity and collective wellbeing.

TSR   Technologies can be useful to reduce human and society sufferings through:
- prevention, early detection, diagnosis, and real-time communication;
- remote care technologies can facilitate flexibility and the capacity of the healthcare system to respond to emergencies promptly;
- telehealth, digital therapeutics, and care navigation enhance the quality of life;
- patients access care services without going physically to hospital facilities.

Value maximization

VBHC   Technologies ensure resilience:
- guaranteeing real-time decision-making and business continuity;
- overcoming fragmentation;
- avoiding duplication of care, time, and cost.

Value co-creation   Digital health is a lever for empowering patients:
- facilitating the exchange with healthcare professionals;
- minimizing barriers;
- providing a more experiential and systemic value creation to patients.

Patient focus

Patient centricity   Patient-centric technologies come into action by:
- monitoring and supporting care with twofold real-time information: clinical outcomes and patients' needs alignment;
- empowering patients and involving them in healthcare provision through remote healthcare technologies (online/mobile patient solutions, telemedicine applications, e-health);
- Healthcare services can be recorded and personal health data guarantee a continuum of care.

Patient experience   Digital health technologies allow:
- measuring patient experience in real time;
- contributing to patient engagement.

Health 4.0 enabled a shift from mass and reactive healthcare to personalized and proactive healthcare (El Saddik et al., 2019) with digital infrastructure able to manage patient data coming from different sources (i.e., smart implants, sensors, and biomedical images), collected through different computer networks, to potentially provide assisted diagnosis by artificial intelligence techniques. In order to activate this process, patients' needs and their evolution should be monitored during the entire healthcare journey/experience (Rubenstein et al., 2014; Cook et al., 2015).

In conclusion, the digital healthcare revolution is foreseen to impact how traditional care is perceived. Every process, organization, and people will be affected by this change that will be centered on patients' needs, consistently with sustainable development. It will imply a redefinition of value provided to patients, their experience, stakeholders' interactions, and collaboration with positive consequences on patients' wellbeing.

REFERENCES

Ciasullo, M. V., Manna, R., Cavallone, M., & Palumbo, R. (2020). Envisioning the future of health systems: Exploratory insights from European countries. *Futures, 121,* 102585.

Cook, N., Hollar, L., Isaac, E., Paul, L., Amofah, A., & Shi, L. (2015). Patient experience in health center medical homes. *Journal of Community Health, 40*(6), 1155–1164.

du Plessis, D., Sake, J. K., Halling, K., Morgan, J., Georgieva, A., & Bertelsen, N. (2017). Patient centricity and pharmaceutical companies: Is it feasible? *Therapeutic Innovation & Regulatory Science, 51*(4), 460–467.

El Saddik, A., Hossain, M. S., & Kantarci, B. (Eds.). (2019). *Connected health in smart cities.* Springer Nature.

Markwart, H., Bomba, F., Menrath, I., Brenk-Franz, K., Ernst, G., Thyen, U., et al. (2020). Assessing empowerment as multidimensional outcome of a patient education program for adolescents with chronic conditions: A latent difference score model. *PLoS One, 15*(4), e0230659.

Rozenblum, R., Greaves, F., & Bates, D. W. (2017). The role of social media around patient experience and engagement. *BMJ Quality & Safety, 26*(10), 845–848.

Rubenstein, L. V., Stockdale, S. E., Sapir, N., Altman, L., Dresselhaus, T., Salem-Schatz, S., Vivell, S., Ovretveit, J., Hamilton, A. B., & Yano, E. M. (2014). A patient-centered primary care practice approach using evidence-based quality improvement: Rationale, methods, and early assessment of implementation. *Journal of General Internal Medicine, 29*(2), 589–597.

Printed in the United States
by Baker & Taylor Publisher Services

Printed in the United States
by Baker & Taylor Publisher Services